NORMAN LONDON

NORMAN LONDON

BY

WILLIAM FITZ STEPHEN

NORMAN LONDON: AN ESSAY

BY

SIR FRANK STENTON

INTRODUCTION BY

F. DONALD LOGAN

ITALICA PRESS
NEW YORK
1990

ITALICA PRESS, INC.
595 Main Street
New York, New York 10044

Library of Congress Cataloging-in-Publication Data

Fitzstephen, William, d. 1190?
    [Descriptio nobilissimae civitatis Londoniae. English]
    Norman London / William Fitz Stephen. Norman London: an essay /
by Sir Frank Stenton ; introduction by F. Donald Logan.
    p.   cm.
    Originally published in 1934 as Historical Association leaflets nos. 93, 94.
    Includes bibliographical references.
    ISBN 0-934977-19-4
    1. London (England) — History — To 1500 — Sources. 2. Great
Britain — History — Norman period, 1066-1154 — Sources. 3. Great
Britain — History — Norman period, 1066-1154. 4. Normans — England — London — History — Sources. 5. London (England) — History
— To 1500. 6. Normans — England — London — History. I. Stenton,
F. M. (Frank Merry), 1880-1967. Norman London. 1990. II. Title.
DA680.F58 1990
942.1'202 — dc20   89-46223

ISBN: 978-0-934977-19-7
Printed in the U.S.A. and E.U.

5 4 3

CONTENTS

ILLUSTRATIONS

PREFACE

Norman London is a collection of important studies presented to give a full picture of this city after the Norman Conquest of 1066. The collection is built around a text from sometime before 1183 in which William Fitz Stephen describes the City of London, its topography, monuments, trades, industries and population. It is a vivid eye-witness account by one of its own citizens that records the daily life and urban pastimes of its people. This text, originally written as an introduction to Fitz Stephen's *Life of Thomas Becket,* is unique among medieval texts for its attention to the sounds and sights of a cityscape.

Fitz Stephen's *Description* was translated by H.E. Butler, Professor of Latin at the University of London, and originally published by The Historical Association (London) in 1934. This was accompanied by several sections of notes, which have been integrated in this edition into one set of end-notes to the text. This *Description* appeared as a companion piece to Sir Frank M. Stenton's important essay, *Norman London,* which is also published here as it originally appeared.

Stenton, one of the most famous and influential of twentieth-century British historians, was a graduate of Keble College, Oxford (1902) with first-class honours in history. He was chair of

Modern History at Reading University College until 1946 and the husband of Doris Mary (Parsons) Stenton. His major works include *The First Century of English Feudalism 1066-1166* (1932) and *Anglo-Saxon England* (1943). In addition to its appearance here and in the Historical Association Leaflets, Stenton's essay has been reprinted in *Social Life in Early England* (Geoffrey Barraclough, ed., London: Routledge & Kegan Paul, 1960, pp. 179-207); and *Preparatory to Anglo-Saxon England* (Doris M. Stenton, ed., Oxford: Clarendon, 1970, pp. 23-47).

This text on Norman London by Fitz Stephen and Stenton's essay were supplemented in the Historical Association leaflets 93 and 94 by three extremely helpful documents: a Bibliographical Note, a Map of London under Henry II by Marjorie B. Honeybourne, with annotations by E. Jeffries Davis of the University of London.

The present edition includes a new introduction by F. Donald Logan, Professor of History at Emmanuel College, Boston. Professor Logan has also provided a new bibliography to bring the Bibliographical Note of the original edition up-to-date. The original map, which was included in the leaflets as an oversized foldout, has been reduced and is reproduced and electronically enhanced in substantially the same form. A detail of the general map showing the parish churches within the city is also presented here. The volume concludes with a glossary of terms and an index.

The Historical Association has generously provided permission to reproduce the material from the original leaflets. Mrs. Madeline Stiles, Association Secretary, was most helpful in making this publication possible.

INTRODUCTION

BY

F. Donald Logan

The London of the Normans, introduced in these pages by Sir Frank Stenton and described by the contemporary writer William Fitz Stephen, was an ancient city but not as ancient as Londoners in the Norman age believed.

Fitz Stephen (below, p. 55), repeating Geoffrey of Monmouth, who, in turn, was repeating an older myth, gave London an origin that rivalled and, indeed, surpassed the legendary founding of Rome. London was founded, he wrote, by Trojans, not by Aeneas who, guided by his goddess mother, went to Italy, but by other Trojans who sailed to this island and up its principal waterway, and there established this city, another Troy, founded by Brutus before Romulus and Remus founded Rome. Thus, London existed not only before the Romans (i.e., Caesar and Claudius) but before Rome itself. Alas, neither is true. London before Rome is the stuff of make-believe and wishful thinking, a myth that died a fairly early death. London before the Romans has long persisted. Scraps of evidence have been seized upon, enlarged beyond reason, to sustain the view that before the coming of the Romans there existed a settlement of Britons on the north bank of the River Thames at the site of London. As early as

1929 Sir Mortimer Wheeler pronounced the death of such a view, but the body is not yet buried. No evidence has emerged to suggest a settlement at this site, and the overwhelming weight of scholarly opinion concludes that London was founded by the Romans on a site where there was no previous settlement.

Of course, there had been human activity in the lower Thames valley for centuries before the Romans. In the ninth or eighth century there seems to have been a center at Egham. Other sites in the lower Thames valley no doubt replaced Egham. For the century or so before the coming of the Romans there are signs of a cult center at Hounslow Heath. Some bronze objects have been found between Brentford and Waterloo. Trade with the Belgic people, at least in part, used the Thames. Also, the lack of a settlement at what later became London does not imply that that area had absolutely no human habitation: it means instead that there was no *settlement* at this place.

Where is the site and why was it chosen by the Romans? These are two related questions. In A.D. 43 the water level of the River Thames was about fourteen feet lower than it is now. At this particular place nineteen miles upstream from the estuary the river was fordable. There may indeed have been existing fording places further upstream – for example, at Westminster – but the Britons probably had these places well fortified during this campaign. And, so, a bridge was built, at first a pontoon bridge at river level, one which could rise and fall with the tide, and, then, within seven years or so, another bridge which was supported so that it remained above tidal level. In order to defend this crucial crossing of the river and to allow the Roman army access to the north a garrison was stationed at the north bridgehead. Although archaeologists have recently unearthed important indications of the nature of the south bridgehead (at Southwark), there can be no doubt that the Roman garrison was on the north bank of the Thames.

From garrison to city took but a short time and by the time the Roman historian Tacitus was writing (by 115), the circuit of the city was four and a half miles and the city required – if one can believe this Roman historian – a thousand men to defend. The Roman city had come into being, and the Romans called it Londinium. No one knows why this name was given. The word must have a native origin, but what? Possibly the name of a local farm or the description of a local topographical feature. Whatever its source, London (in one form or other of the word) she has been called from the first century.

No period in the history of the island is so veiled in darkness as the period from c.450 – c.600, and the darkness falls particularly over London. The departure of the Romans and the coming of Germanic peoples (whom Bede called Angles, Saxons and Jutes) are seen only hazily. It has been suggested that London was abandoned at this time. Indeed, very little of Roman London has survived, neither the street plan nor the great buildings of this Roman provincial metropolis. Even if the actual site had some continuous settlement, London's great significance from after the initial conquest had been as a trading center, as the principal entrepôt in trade linking the continent with England, and whatever might have happened on the site, this mercantile vitality clearly did not survive and, only after several centuries, was it to be reestablished. When the veil over England begins to lift in the seventh century, London was a Saxon town, the center of the Middle Saxons.

As the Germanic tribes became more settled in England, London was to come under the overlordship of the kings of Mercia. There are some indications of this arrangement from the last quarter of the seventh century and, by the end of Ethelbald's reign (d.757), the Mercians had full authority over what had been the lands of the Middle Saxons: London was a Mercian town, its commercial significance gradually being realized.

This appearance of a Saxon London from the seventh century should not lead us to conclude that Saxon London rose on the site of Roman London. Such does not seem to have been the case. Recent archaeological evidence reveals a fairly substantial Saxon settlement from the seventh century, which peaked in the eighth and disappeared (probably moved) in the ninth, a settlement not *within* but *outside* the Roman walls, between the west wall and today's Westminster. The evidence suggests that this Strand (or Aldwych) site was, in fact, the site of early Saxon London and that it was not till the ninth century that the Saxons moved the focus of their commercial interests to the Roman site. When Pope Gregory I (relying on old memories of London's significance in Roman times) tried unsuccessfully to establish a metropolitan see at London in the early seventh century, the London referred to was apparently this early Saxon settlement to the west of what had been the Roman city, and, when its cathedral was built some time after 604, it was built, as have been its successors, on the hill immediately to the east.

The place played by London during the periods of the Viking attacks is still being revealed to us.

Viking campaigns are generally associated with the North, the Midlands, East Anglia and Wessex, and not with the London area. This is not entirely true. There were lightning Viking raids on London in 842 and, again, in 851. With apparent ease the Viking leader Halfdan went to London in 871 to winter there. The Vikings minted coins there and probably stayed on beyond 872, possibly till Alfred occupied London in the mid-880s (probably earlier than 886, the traditional date for the Alfredan occupation). When the Vikings came there again, in the early eleventh century, London held off an attack (1009), and, in face of the collapse of the English defense, laid perhaps unfairly at the feet of King Ethelred, London submitted to the man who would be king, the Dane Swein (1013). And, in a brilliant move in 1013 after London had reverted to English control, Swein's son Cnut bypassed London Bridge (via a hastily dug canal south of the bridge) and was able to lay siege the city from the west, and London became his.

When news reached London of King Harold's defeat at Hastings on October 14, 1066, the full impact of this news was not realized. A second line of defence, it was thought, might be set up before London: the country was not defeated. In the event, no defense would be successful. As his conquering army reached the Southwark end of London Bridge, William found it defended and, rather than destroy the city, he decided to capture the regions around London, thus encircling the city and forcing its surrender. Surrender, indeed, London did. The circumstances are variously reported, and, according to one account, it was only when the Norman army could be seen approaching that London accepted the inevitable. Thus, Norman London, the subject of this book, began.

NORMAN LONDON

BY

Sir Frank Stenton

For the study of Norman London there is no lack of material, but it is material of an unusual kind. We must, it would seem, for ever lack that detailed description of the city which should fill the 126th folio of the first volume of Domesday Book. For such a description there is no substitute. We cannot make the vaguest profitable guess at the number of houses in the eleventh century city, still less at the number of its inhabitants, and the considerable body of charter evidence which we possess throws only an uncertain light on the London which resisted the Conqueror. On the other hand, Professor Liebermann has rescued from association with other texts a city custumal of Stephen's time, and no other town can show the like. Mr. Round has established the family relationships of many leading citizens, and traced the dealings of the city with the king. Miss Bateson has analysed the fragments of ancient law implied in the liberties which the men of London claimed. Every contemporary historian of the twelfth century was forced to refer to London, and to illustrate, if only incidentally, the importance of the

1

city and the political interests of its citizens. Writers of this kind occasionally supply important facts for which there is no evidence in local records. The materials for the history of Norman London may often be hard to interpret, but they are at least copious.

The city of London stood alone above other English towns in wealth and power, and its citizens were very conscious of the fact. Their remarkable statement in 1135 that to them it belonged of right to choose a king for England[1] was only the most dramatic assertion of their position. They were known collectively as barons, and this style was allowed them by the clerks who wrote the writs of William II and Henry I.[2] The city was "refugium et propugnaculum regni"[3]; it could be maintained that its liberties were necessary for the well-being of the whole kingdom. London was a political and financial power on which a wise king would keep a careful eye, and its citizens were alert to draw advantage from royal embarrassments. They could extort the legitimation of their Commune from Count John, could play off the empress Matilda against King Stephen. London, to them, was more than a city, it was a commonwealth.

This pre-eminence of London was no new thing. No other town, not Lincoln nor Winchester, included so many moneyers striking pennies for Edward the Confessor or Cnut. But as the history of London is traced backward beyond 1066, its distinctive significance ceases to be merely that of a great urban centre. London under the successors of Alfred is revealed, sporadically but unmistakably, as in some way the head of a rural district indeterminate but wide. "This is the decree that the bishops and reeves who belong to London, eorl and ceorl, have published and established with pledges in our peace gild, in addition to the laws that were given at Grateley, Exeter, and Thundersfield."[4] This sentence is enough to prove that external magnates as well as humble folk were regarded for some purpose as subject to an authority established in London. Probably the twelfth-century translator of these laws was right in considering that purpose to be judicial. In any case, it is reasonable to connect this passage with the reference to the lands that "belonged" to London and Oxford, over which Edward the Elder assumed rule upon the death of earl Ethelred of the Mercians.[5] And so it is easier to understand how in 1097 shires could owe work to London,[6] and how, in the next century, Londoners could enjoy ancient hunting rights in Middlesex, Surrey, the Chiltern Hills,[7] and, according to one informant, Kent, as far as the Cray.[8] This privilege is suggestive; kings may well have enjoined that men should all come for justice from a wide region to some central town, but the right of hunting over more than two whole shires is likely to be a survival. It was certainly a reality: the Conqueror found it necessary to forbid the Londoners to take stags, hinds, or roe deer within archbishop Lanfranc's manor of Harrow.[9] It would be hard to name any period in later Anglo-Saxon history in which the origin of such a right would seem plausible; and where all is speculation, we may perhaps derive this privilege from a time in which the Middle Saxons were still a separate people, and London was their "metropolis."

It was inevitable that the Conqueror should attempt to conciliate the men of this ancient and formidable city. Early in his reign, though not, as has sometimes been thought, in its first weeks, he addressed a writ to William the bishop, Geoffrey (de Mandeville) the portreeve, and all the borough community within London, French and English, informing them of his will that they should enjoy the rights which had belonged to them in King Edward's day, that their property should descend to their children, and that no one should do them injury.[10] The interest of this famous document is political rather than constitutional, for it amounts to little more than a general confirmation of the conditions of 1066 to the men of London. It is the letter of a foreign king who knows that his throne will never be safe while the men of his greatest city are disaffected, and hopes to secure their good will by assuring them that he will respect their privileges and property and will protect them against aggressors. The most curious feature of the charter is the fact that the king uses the dual number in addressing the men to whom he is confirming their pre-Conquest rights. Translated strictly, the first clause of the charter reads, "I will that ye both be worthy of all the rights of which ye both were worthy in King Edward's day." In using this method of expression, the king is clearly distinguishing between the bishop of London on the one hand and the portreeve and citizens on the other. Unusual expressions like this always mean something definite, and the present example can only mean that the Conqueror's charter to London was deliberately phrased so as to cover the bishop as it covered the citizens.[11]

The clearest proof of the insecurity of the king's hold on London at the beginning of his reign lies in the castles which he built, or allowed to be built, there. The city had submitted unwillingly, and the king's first care was to erect fortifications which would keep it in obedience. Immediately after his coronation he moved to Barking, and spent some days there "while certain strongholds were made in the town against the fickleness of the vast and fierce populace."[12] There can be no serious doubt that one of these strongholds consisted of elementary defences of moat and bank on the site, just within the southeast angle of the Wall, where the White Tower was to be built in the following years. Historians seem to be agreed in attributing the beginnings of the Tower of London to this time, but they have laid comparatively little stress on the evidence which shows that one if not two fortresses arose under the Norman Kings in the extreme south-west of the city. William Fitz Stephen mentions two very strong castles as existing in his time in the west,[13] and two castles in the same quarter are recorded by other authorities. The better known of them was the Baynard's Castle which has left its name to one of the largest wards of the city. The name must have arisen early in the Norman period, for it preserves the surname of Ralf Baignard, a great tenant in chief in eastern England in 1086, and William Baignard, the last English baron of this family, was deprived of his inheritance in 1110.[14] It is suggestive that another important eastern baron, Geoffrey de Mandeville, received the custody of the Tower from William the Conqueror. Soon after William Baignard's disinheritance,

Henry I gave Baynard's Castle to a member of a third family powerful in eastern England, Robert fitz Richard of Clare, and as long as it was defensible it remained in the hands of his descendants, giving much influence in London to the most famous of them, the Robert fitz Walter who led the baronial opposition to King John.[15]

The history of the second castle on the west of the city, the Montfichet Castle of later records,[16] is obscure. It probably stood between Baynard's Castle and Ludgate, but its exact site is unknown. It played a much smaller part than Baynard's Castle in the history of the city, and there seems to be only one reference to it as a place of military importance. Jordan Fantosme, the author of a contemporary poem on the rebellion of 1173-4, introduces into his narrative a long passage purporting to be a report on conditions in England brought to Henry II in Normandy by the bishop of Winchester. At the end,[17] the king asks how his barons of London are behaving. The bishop tells him that they are the most loyal people in his realm, and that all of sufficient age are under arms, but that Gilbert de Munfichet has strengthened his castle, and says that the "Clarreaus" are allied with him. To this the king replies, "God have mercy, and protect the barons of my city of London." Gilbert de Munfichet was lord of a large fief in eastern England, of which the head was Stansted Mountfitchet in Essex. He was a cousin of Walter fitz Robert fitz Richard of Clare, the lord of Baynard's Castle, and it is safe to identify the "Clarreaus," whose alliance Gilbert was claiming, with Walter fitz Robert and the great family to which he belonged.[18] For the history of London, the especial interest of the passage lies in the importance which it assigns to Gilbert de Munfichet's Castle. It is evident that, at the moment, this obscure fortress, under its hostile lord, was a serious danger to the king's hold upon the city.

From the time of its foundation it is probable that the possession of Baynard's Castle gave to its lord a position of official authority within the city. In 1100 or 1101 Henry I addressed to Hugh of Buckland the sheriff, William Baignard, and the king's ministers of London, a writ confirming to archbishop Anselm's men visiting or resident in London the privileges which archbishop Lanfranc's men had enjoyed.[19] It may be taken as certain that William Baignard was no less responsible than the sheriff and the king's ministers for seeing that the king's writ was carried into effect. But there are few early documents which illustrate the official responsibilities of the lords of Baynard's Castle, and there is a distinct air of antiquarian reconstruction about some of the later evidence. By the reign of Edward I, Baynard's Castle had ceased to be a fortress, and in 1275 Robert fitz Walter II received licence to alienate it for the site of a house of Dominican Friars. But he retained the privileges in the city which had belonged to him before the alienation, and a statement of his case in 1303 brings out the very interesting fact that the earlier lords of Baynard's Castle had been commanders of the host of the citizens of London.[20] A fourteenth century record can only be used with caution for conditions in the Norman period. The case put forward by Robert fitz Walter assumes that the chief magistrate of the city will be a mayor, and states that the horse which the lord of Baynard's

Castle receives as part of his fee should be "saddled with the arms of the said Robert." Indications like these suggest the thirteenth century rather than the Norman age. But the case includes features which have an ancient air – notably the reservation that Robert should only receive a hundred shillings for each town or castle besieged by the host, even if the siege lasted for a whole year, – and there is direct evidence that the essential part of the fitz Walter claim was recognised in the Norman period. Early in the thirteenth century, a jury reported that none but the owners of certain privileged properties could draw fishing-nets in the Thames between Baynard's Castle and Staines without the licence of the lord or constable of Baynard's Castle.[21] The jury based their finding on the result of a plea held in or before 1136 at St. Paul's before the king's council, which gave judgment that the lordship of the water of Thames between these points belonged to the lord of Baynard's Castle as the king's standard-bearer and the keeper – *procurator* – of the city. In view of this definite statement, there is no need to doubt the antiquity of the custom underlying Robert fitz Walter's claim that in time of war he should come to the west door of St. Paul's, mounted, with eleven other knights, and there receive the banner of the city, that he should then direct the choice of a marshall for the city host, order the summoning of the commons, and finally, in the priory of the Holy Trinity, Aldgate, choose two discreet men from each ward to keep the city safely.

It is easy to underestimate the part which must have been played by the army of London in the civil wars of the Norman period, for its activities are rarely mentioned by contemporaries. It is therefore worth noting that on one occasion, in Stephen's reign, it intervened in a campaign with results which affected the general history of the country. In the summer of 1145, Robert, earl of Gloucester, built a castle at Faringdon in Berkshire, which if held would have maintained easy communication between his base in the Severn valley and his important outpost of Wallingford. Its capture was worth a great effort on Stephen's part, and a contemporary historian states explicitly that the king brought for its reduction *Lundonensium terribilem et numerosum exercitum*.[22] The castle was taken, and to the author who has been quoted its fall marked the turning-point in Stephen's fortunes. It is only a single writer who mentions the share which the Londoners had in this success. But it is clear that the "formidable and large army of the men of London" was something more than a historic survival in Stephen's reign.

The essential link between the military and the civil administration of London was formed by the city wards. In time of war, they formed the basis of the organisation for the defence of the city, and they provided for the keeping of watch within its boundaries in time of peace. We have no direct information about these divisions earlier than the reign of Henry I, when twenty of them are mentioned by name in a survey of the London property belonging to St. Paul's Cathedral.[23] Few of the wards in this early list can be identified with any certainty. Its "warda fori" and "warda Alegate" can safely be equated with the later wards of Cheap and Aldgate, and its "warda Brocesgange" preserves the Old English name of the division now known as Walbrook ward.[24] But each of the other wards in the list is defined by the name of an individual, presumably the alderman who presided over it, and descriptions such as "warda Haconis" or "warda Radulfi filii Liuiue" are of little use for purposes of local identification. It is probable that under Henry I as in the thirteenth century the city was divided into twenty four wards,[25] and it seems certain that each ward had its own court, the wardmoot of later records, which corresponded in function to the court of a rural hundred. The profits of justice done in these assemblies were the king's, though already in the Norman period innumerable properties had passed from the jurisdiction of the ward, its alderman, and his officers, under the authority of privileged private land-owners, the lords of sokes. But the rise of the sokes should not obscure the significance of the ward as the fundamental unit of local justice and administration in Norman London.

A mong the institutions which covered the whole city the folkmoot is first in dignity,[26] as doubtless it was first in age. If it did not, as one Londoner of the twelfth century liked to think, exist already in the time of Arthur, the most famous king of Britain, many facts point to its antiquity.[27] It was the proper scene for the proclamation of outlawry: in this respect it ranked with the provincial shire court. The burden of suit fell upon all men of London; no individual summons was necessary, it was assumed that everyone would hear the great bell of St. Paul's which rang for the meeting. Three sessions only were held in the year – at Michaelmas, Christmas, and Midsummer. Presumably the sheriff presided, as in the analogous shire court; at any rate, the Michaelmas session met to know who the new sheriff should be, and to hear his command. The Christmas meeting took cognisance of keeping the wards; at Midsummer, the heat of the season led to recurrent provisions against fire. These are ancient provisions, and essential to the life of any town; the complicated business of a great city which was a distributing centre for all England, in which land changed owners with unusual frequency, was conducted, not in the folkmoot, but in the husting.

The chief difficulty in the history of this body lies in its name. The word Husting is certainly of Scandinavian origin, and at first, apparently, meant an assembly of a great man's dependents, meeting within doors, though it had acquired a more general sense by the eleventh century.[28] The London husting is first mentioned in a Latin translation of an Old English private document of the late tenth century,[29] which refers to two silver cups of twelve marks, "by the weight of the husting of London." If this reference can be trusted – and it would be a pointless invention – it shows that the London husting was in being before the conquest of England by Swegn and Cnut. It must therefore have arisen in the century following the Scandinavian occupation of London in Alfred's time, but the circumstances of its origin are still obscure. It is possible that the husting was created by the ninth century Scandinavian occupants of London. But we have no direct evidence of any Scandinavian immigration into London so considerable as of itself to produce a new form of public assembly. London passed again under English lordship as early as 886, and although little is known about its inhabitants during the next forty years, the names of London moneyers in the tenth century point unmistakeably to their English origin. In these circumstances it seems probable that the Scandinavian influence which produced the husting resulted from long-continued intercourse rather than from sudden immigration, that, in fact, the husting arose to meet the needs of English citizens who were in constant association with Scandinavian traders. It is significant that the earliest references to the husting mention it in connexion with a particular standard weight of precious metal. At a later time, the husting was much occupied with matters of commercial regulation, and it may well be that this side of its activity was original.

In the twelfth century it met every Monday in the Guildhall. Like the men who attended the ancient local assemblies of the country, its suitors sat upon four benches.[30] It was the recognised court for civil business, for pleas of debt, for disputes about land: a wise grantee would make some formal delivery of his gift before the husting. In contrast with the immemorial duty of attendance at the folkmoot, a special summons was necessary to enforce an answer in a suit before the husting. It had cognisance of cases to which foreign merchants were parties; it controlled weights and measures. The volume of its business must have been immense. Within the husting we can just see that the aldermen form a class apart; they are expected to know the law; it is their duty to speak right. In the Norman age, it was possible, and it may have been usual, for an alderman to be followed in office by his son,[31] and in this respect, as in the matter of their legal knowledge, the Anglo-Norman aldermen of London show a definite resemblance to the eleventh century lawmen of Lincoln and Stamford. In these aldermen, who adjudicate in the husting and are at the same time in charge of wards,[32] we are most likely to find those elder citizens who from time to time appear in the twelfth century evidence.

Their memory still survives in the name of a city street. West of the site occupied by the present Guildhall, its medieval predecessor stood near to the street known as Aldermanbury already in the early twelfth century.[33] Despite some uncertainty as to the original form of the name,[34] early spellings suggest that it represents an Old English *ealdormanna burh,* fortified enclosure[35] of the aldermen. It can hardly be a mere coincidence that a street bearing this name ran close to the hall where the aldermen of the city sat as the leading members of the husting. This local connexion at once raises a difficult question as to the nature of the gild which gave its name to the Guildhall. No certain answer can be given to this question, but the Guildhall first appears under Henry I in an incidental way which shows that it was no new thing at that date,[36] and the local connexion with Aldermanbury suggests that we may have in its name a trace of an association of aldermen, formed in Old English times, and obsolete already in the early Norman period.

One ancient association of the same kind undoubtedly came to an end in this period. Late in the eleventh century, we obtain our first reference to a body of men called the *Cnihtena gild* of London.[37] William II and Henry I confirmed to them their gild and its land with all its privileges as they had enjoyed them in the time of King Edward and the Conqueror. These confirmations reveal the gild as still a reality in the earliest years of the twelfth century, but in 1125 its members in return for spiritual benefits gave all its lands to the newly-founded priory of the Holy Trinity, Aldgate. The names of the men who made this gift have been preserved, and a comparison of the list with other London documents shows that they included some of the leading citizens of the time. Among the few members of the gild not hitherto mentioned otherwise in connexion with the city "Wlward le Douerisshe," the second on the list, was one of the earliest benefactors to Reading Abbey, to which, as Wlward Dourensis, he gave land and houses in London.[38] The gild itself was remarkably well endowed, for its lands included the large tract outside the east wall of the city, afterwards called Portsoken Ward.[39] But its origin and character can only be matters of conjecture. The transference of its property to the priory of the Holy Trinity virtually proves that whatever its history had been, it had become essentially an association for religious purposes by the twelfth century. Its name brings it into comparison with the gilds of *cnihts* which existed in the Norman age[40] at Winchester and Canterbury, and the fact that the Canterbury gild is mentioned in a charter of the mid ninth century shows that such associations existed already in the pre-Alfredian period. The *cnihtas* by whom they were formed should not be regarded as a military class.[41] The Old English word *cniht* meant a servant or retainer, not a warrior, and in a document written in English between 1093 and 1109, the Canterbury *cnihts* are expressly called cnihts of the chapmens' gild.[42] There is no such clear evidence for the nature of the London *cnihtena gild*. It is, on the whole, most probable that the original *cnihtas* of London were responsible servants of magnates owning property in London,[43] appointed to supply their lords with goods coming to the London market, and that, in course of time, independent traders entering the association changed the character of its membership while enrolling themselves under its ancient name. But we only see the London *cnihtena gild* in the very last years of its existence, when, whatever its origin, it was a wealthy association of prominent London citizens.

The estate of the *cnihtena gild* which became Portsoken Ward was only distinguished by its size and its position outside the walls from a great number of private franchises scattered over the whole city. The distinctive feature of London justice in the Norman age is the influence of such private liberties, the sokes. The urban immunity attains its greatest English development in London, for in other towns the landowner who held houses with sac and soc seems rarely to have held a permanent court for his tenants.[44] In part, the number and persistence of the London sokes was due to the commercial importance of the city. Access to the London market through a house in or near the city was desired by many country landowners in the eleventh century. London, like other towns, contained houses appurtenant to rural estates. The Domesday description of Surrey[45] supplies numerous instances. The archbishop of Canterbury had seventeen *mansuræ* in London belonging to Mortlake, the bishop of Bayeux had one *masura* belonging to Banstead, Miles Crispin had lost to earl Roger of Shrewsbury thirteen *masuræ* belonging to Beddington, count Eustace of Boulogne had fifteen *masuræ* in London and Southwark belonging to "Wachelestede," now Godstone, Richard fitz Gilbert had seven *mansuræ* in London and Southwark belonging to Bletchingley, the king himself had thirteen "burgesses" in London belonging to Bermondsey. Great monasteries like Ramsey, Chertsey, Ely, and Abingdon acquire property in London, and in the eleventh century some of them obtain royal writs which confer powers of jurisdiction.[46] That most of our early information relates to monastic properties is only due to the better preservation of ecclesiastical muniments, for the lay owner of a soke is prominent in the century after the Conquest. We read of the sokes of the honours of Huntingdon, Peverel, and Mortain,[47] the soke of Gilbert of Torigni,[48] the soke of the earl of Gloucester,[49] the queen's soke. Gisulf, a royal scribe under Henry I, held a soke of the Archbishop of Canterbury.[50] The impression is produced that most barons of superior consequence possessed a privileged estate in London; the conception of immunity so governed men's ideas of local justice that those portions of the city outside the jurisdiction of a private court are described collectively in the twelfth century as the king's soke.[51]

But London citizens might themselves possess rights of jurisdiction over their properties in the city. It has been conjectured that the Ealdred who gave his name to Aldersgate was an immunist; the same may be true of the original Billing of Billingsgate. These sokes presented a most formidable obstacle to the growth of any ubiquitous city jurisdiction. No dweller within a soke might be arrested in his house or penthouse; or anywhere except in the middle of the road. Distraint within a soke was a complicated business, only to be accomplished after invoking the soke reeve. Temporary dwellers within a soke owed nothing by way of customary payment to anyone except the lord of the soke.[52] All disputes between the men of the same soke would be settled privately, and Norman London was still in the archaic atmosphere of the weregild and the monetary emendation for personal violence. The reeve, in the London soke, plays the part of rural steward as the immunist's official. It is interesting to note that when the word sokeman appears in the London custumals it means, as in its rare appearances in West Scandinavian law, the reeve, the executive officer of a court who carries through its judgments.

The sokes of Norman London have left their impression on the later nomenclature of the city in the name of Portsoken Ward, that great extramural soke or liberty of the priory of the Holy Trinity, Aldgate, which has already been mentioned in connexion with the *cnihtena gild*. It is a curious name, which has long aroused interest, and its exact significance is not easily determined. Translated strictly, "portsoken" means simply "town soke,"[53] and it has sometimes been assumed to refer to some special authority over the city possessed by the members of the *cnihtena gild,* its first lords. But

17

the *cnihtena gild* was not in any sense the governing body of the city, and it has recently become apparent that the word port soke was applied to other London franchises beside the famous one outside the walls. In the Pipe Roll of 1194, William de Ste. Mère Eglise renders account of 21 shillings *de Portsocha Willemi de M un*.[54] A similar entry occurs in each of the following years, and in 1197 this liberty appears both as the "soke" and the "port soke" of William de Mohun,[55] whose lands throughout this period were in the king's hands. It would therefore seem that soke and port soke were interchangeable terms, and as there was nothing exceptional in the London liberty of the Mohun lords of Dunster, it follows that any one of the innumerable franchises in the city might have been described as a port soke. In view of this identity the chief difficulties attending the name Portsoken Ward disappear. It simply means "the soke ward"; a description which is curiously indefinite, but agrees very well with the unique position of Portsoken Ward. Few London wards corresponded even approximately in area to sokes, and Portsoken Ward was the only one of them in which the lord of the soke became *ex officio* alderman.[56]

With the soke, the sphere of private jurisdiction, is closely associated the defensible house, the *burh*. The precincts of St. Paul's constituted such a place of defence; Æthelflæd, widow of king Edmund I, about 975, left the reversion of certain lands "to Paul's *burh* at London, to the bishop's house."[57] The idea of the private stronghold was familiar in tenth century society; one famous text would make the possession of such a defensible place a condition of a ceorl's advancement to thegnly rank.[58] In

London, traces of the private defensible house may still be found in local names which end in "bury."[59] Lothbury for example, seems to mean the defensible place of someone whose name began with the Old English name-stem Hloth. The defences whose existence is implied by the word *burh* were doubtless elementary, in most cases probably little more than a walled enclosure around a house.[60] The word is, however, interesting as an indication of the type of dwelling possessed by the greater citizens of early London, and as one of the many Old English local terms which survived the Norman Conquest within and around the city. The Bucherelli, whose name survives in Bucklersbury and is of Italian origin, certainly cannot have been established in London before the Conquest.

N ames like Bucklersbury symbolise the union of English and foreign elements which determined the character of London society in the Norman age. The foreign element has always been emphasised by historians, and, indeed, so fully that the older and stronger native influences have sometimes been allowed to fall into the background of the picture. It is well to remember that personal names of English origin will almost certainly preponderate in any early post-Conquest list of London citizens. Even in Stephen's time, nearly half the recorded moneyers of London have English names. The English element is dominant in the names of the members of the *cnihtena gild,* and extremely strong in the names of the witnesses to the early London charters of St. Paul's, and in those of the London citizens who presided over wards late in the reign of Henry I. In all this there is nothing peculiar to London. English names lasted long in every ancient English borough. It is much more remarkable that names of this type occur continually in the lists of early canons of St. Paul's Cathedral.[61] It is always hard to discover anything definite as to the personal history of the members of an Anglo-Norman cathedral chapter, but we have clear evidence that at London it included men having a family connexion with the city. In 1104, a woman named Thurgund gave a piece of land to St. Paul's, "by the advice and at the request of Thedebald the canon, whose sons were kinsmen of Thured, her husband."[62] This is a strange way of stating a relationship, but it leaves no doubt as to the local associations of Thedebald the canon. It therefore increases the probability that most of the canons of English name who occur in early lists[63] were connected by family ties with the city. In any case, these names are numerous enough to show that the English elements which prevailed in early Norman London were strongly represented in the chapter of its cathedral.

Under these conditions, it was natural that when the citizens of London obtained a detailed grant of privileges from the king, many of its provisions should have a retrospective appearance. Few records in English municipal history are better known or have had wider influence than the great charter of liberties which Henry I issued to London.[64] The original document had escaped from the custody of the city before the end of John's reign, and has not since been found. Its exact text is uncertain at more than one point, and although it was probably granted between Michaelmas, 1130 and July, 1133, its date cannot be exactly fixed. Nevertheless it defines not merely the king's opinion of the liberties which were the reasonable privilege of his greatest city, but also the citizens' own conception of what the relations between themselves and the king should be. The spirit of the charter is that of the earliest London custumals, demanding a real if limited degree of self-government in matters of finance and justice, and commercial privileges throughout the land. Here, as often in similar documents, it is hard to distinguish between the clauses which grant new privileges and those which merely give new force to existing custom. The king's grant of exemption from fiscal burdens such as Danegeld and the murder fine may well belong to the latter class, and long established practice seems to be receiving fresh sanction in the clauses allowing the citizens of London to take compensation from the merchants of towns where toll has been taken from Londoners, and to recover losses incurred through the default of external debtors by distraint on other individuals belonging to the defaulter's town or village. But indeed the whole tenor of the charter is conservative. The citizens are expressly relieved from the necessity of submitting to the new process of trial by battle. If it is a new thing that the citizens themselves shall hold the shrievalty of London and Middlesex at farm, the £300 at which that farm was fixed was the sum recognised in the Conqueror's day, though Henry I himself had increased it in the interval and Henry II was to do so again.[65] The citizens' hunting-rights which the king now confirmed were no new privilege.[66] The confirmation of their sokes to churches, barons, and citizens recognises existing facts. It is an innovation, and a great one, that the citizens shall appoint their own sheriff, but, in himself, this officer simply stands for the Old English portreeve. Many other individual clauses read like definitions of custom against royal encroachments. The king's promise that he will cause the citizens to have their lands, the debts owed to them, and the property which they had taken in pledge, suggests past aggressions on the king's behalf, and a definite acknowledgement that citizens have a case against the king is contained in the clause that he will do right to them in respect of the lands touching which they have made complaint to him. There is clearly a recognition of ancient rights by the king in the provisions that the individual citizen shall only be amerced for emendable offences according to his were of 100 shillings, that he shall answer to pleas of the crown by the oath which shall be adjudged to him in the city, that there shall not be fines for wrongful pleading in the folkmoot or husting, and that no one of the king's or any other household shall be compulsorily entertained within the city. Privileges like these would not seem anachronistic if we read of them in texts coming from the eleventh century. Before long, the Londoners were to enlarge their conceptions of civic autonomy.

But in the Norman age proper the city was well enough accommodated with the institutions and officers it had inherited from King Edward's day: the folkmoot, the husting, the private soke; the sheriff and aldermen. The chief innovation in the government of London before the death of Henry I was the establishment in the city of the local justiciar. He was not peculiar to London; he is addressed in association with the sheriff in royal writs addressed to various counties in the second half of Henry's reign. The justiciarship of London might on occasion be held by a great noble. Geoffrey de Mandeville, at a time when nothing could safely be denied him, obtained the office from Stephen and its confirmation from the Empress Matilda. But Henry I had granted that the justiciar, like the sheriff of London should be chosen by the Londoners from among themselves; and Round showed that three prominent London citizens – Andrew Buchuinte, Osbert Huitdeniers, and Gervase of Cornhill – held the justiciarship of London under Stephen.[67]

The justiciar, in London as elsewhere, stands for a temporary royal experiment. In the Charter of Henry I he is empowered "to keep and plead the pleas of my crown" – that is, to see that all pleas in which the King has a direct interest are properly held and determined. In London, as in other counties, he was certainly superior to the sheriff. In what must be one of the latest references to the justiciar of London, Queen Eleanor writing on her husband's behalf, before 1161, tells the sheriff of London that unless he compels John Bucuinte to warrant certain lands to the monks of Reading, "the king's justiciar of London" will act.[68] The justiciar, in fact, appears in the meagre evidence as the permanent local representative of the king, appointed to control the local authorities of his shire or town, to protect the royal interests in the fiscal profits of justice. His power was short-lived because kings found other and more convenient ways of achieving this end.

The first assertion by the Londoners of a claim wider than the preservation of inherited privilege was made in the establishment of their Commune. With the famous Commune of 1191, from which the later mayoralty descends, we are not here concerned; the events of that year do not belong to Norman London. But just fifty years before this date we obtain a fair amount of evidence that something unusual was happening in London; that the citizens were organising themselves in an unprecedented way. William of Malmesbury, for example, tells us that at the Council of London held after the battle of Lincoln, "the Londoners came and...said that they had been sent by the commune, as they call it, of London...to ask that their lord the king might be freed from prison, and that all the barons who had already been received into their commune very earnestly begged this of the lord legate, and the archbishop and clergy."[69] That the association in question was known and recognised abroad may be inferred from the interesting letter which Archbishop Hugh of Rouen addressed to the illustrious senators, the honoured citizens, and all of the commune of London, giving thanks for their fidelity to King Stephen and expressing the hope that as they have thus given pledges of their liberality and justice, they will also do right in the dispute between Algar the priest and Reading Abbey.[70] When the word *communa* is found in the address of a letter written by a foreign prelate of this period to all the men of a city, it deserves to be taken seriously.

It need not, however, be taken as implying anything approaching the revolution which followed the establishment of a commune in a continental town. London does not take rank in the feudal hierarchy of England between the king and a population holding lands of the city, nor at this time is there any anticipation of the organisation of the mayor and his council which was instituted after 1191. By the establishment of a commune in 1141 we may most reasonably understand that the citizens formed a sworn association for the defence of their liberties: a step particularly wise at a moment when the succession was in question, and the charter of Henry I only a decade old. One trace of continental example may perhaps be found in the admission of barons into the commune; for the barons who were so admitted are clearly distinguished by William of Malmesbury from the citizens themselves. The real interest of the movement is in its proof that the city, for all the variety of tenure and justice which it included, was still a unity, and could on occasion be brought to act as such. When once this idea had taken root, the formal and definite foundation of a permanent commune was only a question of time – a question, to be precise, of just half a century.

This unity in political action must have been facilitated by the fact that the laws of Norman London did not recognise any distinction of inherited status among the citizens. The dignity of those "principes civitatis" who met the Conqueror at Berkhampstead, that of the "elder citizens" who occur from time to time later, seems quite an informal thing resulting from superior wealth, or from the tenure of civic office. Henry I in his charter to the citizens assigns to the man of London without qualification the weregild of a hundred shillings. The fact is remarkable, for this is the weregild of a pre-Conquest *ceorl,* of the early Norman *villanus.*[71] It suggests, not the degradation of the London citizen, but the superior status of the eleventh century villein. We are not without evidence of an earlier state of things. When the Confessor addressed three different writs in favour of Westminster to the burh thegns within London, he was recognising a civic patriciate of birth.[72] But there is no later trace of such a class, either in the London custumals or in any of the writs directed to the city after the Conquest, and Henry I, in his charter to the citizens of London, speaks as if the undifferentiated weregild of one hundred shillings were already well established there.[73] And indeed, the immigration of traders from France and beyond must in any case have strained any specifically English law of ranks to breaking-point.

Already in the Norman age London was no mere regional market. It was a terminal point in the trade route from Constantinople, by the Danube and Regensburg, to the Rhine and the narrow seas. In the obscurity which overhangs all early lines of communication from the East, the London evidence is definite and intelligible. The trade was controlled by the men of lower Lorraine, subjects of the Emperor. They brought to London goldsmiths' work, precious stones, cloth from Constantinople and Regensburg, fine linen and coats of mail from Mainz, also wine. The king, through his chamberlain, and in view of the sheriff of London, had the right of pre-emption over all these things. After him the men of London might buy what they wished, then the men of Oxford, then those of Winchester, then all were admitted to purchase.

The valuable trade in pepper, cummin, and wax was also in the hands of the Emperor's men. Danish and Norwegian merchants had the right of dwelling in the city for a year; presumably, as in later times, they brought timber, sail cloth, and such like things, though it may be that they also connected London with the Northern trade line across Russia to the East.[74] With the Norwegians one writer[75] associates the Russians, by whom he means men of the Swedish colony at Novgorod, not yet absorbed by the Slavonic peoples around them. They brought furs and marten skins. The same writer's reference to Arabs and Ethiopians is probably a rhetorical lapse. No laws relating expressly to Norman merchants are recorded in the twelfth century; they were the king's subjects. But Henry II, as Duke of Normandy, confirmed to the men of Rouen their port of Dowgate, as they had held it in the Confessor's time, and freed them from all dues in London except those on wine, and on that indefinite fat fish which is variously interpreted as sturgeon, porpoise, and whale.[76] There is much probability in the suggestion that commercial rivalry led the compilers of London customs to ignore the Flemings outright. Edward the Confessor had given a wharf in London to the Church of St. Peter of Ghent, and the Flemings are seen established in London by royal authority in the charter by which Henry II gave to the men of St. Omer the right to choose lodgings where they would, to sell their goods without view of justiciar or sheriff and without paying dues for their exposure, to go to fairs and markets throughout England.[77] Perhaps the very extent of these liberties measures the opposition of the city to Flemish immigration.

From no other English town have we evidence of so considerable a body of trade at this early date. But it is only right to observe that already at the beginning of the eleventh century or earlier London was being visited by merchants from just the same countries which are represented there under Henry I.[78] The men of Rouen were already selling their wine and their fat fish. The men of Flanders, Ponthieu, Normandy, France – of Huy, Liège, Nivelle – the Emperor's men, the Danes, were already seeking the port. The idea that the Norman Conquest was followed by a revolutionary expansion of the trade of London receives little support from the evidence. We may certainly believe in a considerable entry of French and Flemish merchants, though with the reservation that a very high proportion of London citizens in the early twelfth century bear English names or descend from ancestors who bore them.[79] We must make full allowance for the influence of the unusual quiet of England in attracting foreign traders. Even so, the trade of Norman London was mainly due to geographical facts, which are not affected by foreign conquest.

These facts have often been stated.[80] All of them are subordinate to the essential condition that the Thames could be bridged, that permanent habitations could arise on its banks, at a point where it was still tidal. London is the very type of those towns which arise at a river crossing. London Bridge, a wooden structure in the Norman period, was no insuperable barrier to sea-going vessels, which would commonly go to hythe above it. Queenhithe, the Etheredeshithe of early records, one of the chief hythes of the Norman city, was above the bridge. But it was the first serious obstacle in the navigation of the river. The Thames at London has the function of an arm of the narrow seas extended into the heart of the country. From no other point would foreign wares so conveniently be distributed over the Midlands, and on two occasions the Thames entry has attracted a convergence of roads to London. That the Roman system radiated from the city is the most obvious fact in the geography of the province. Of the general system of English roads in the Norman age our ignorance is almost complete; but when in the fourteenth century we obtain some adequate evidence upon this head,[81] we can trace a system which has fallen away from the Roman lines but still turns upon London. References in twelfth century charters to a *Via Londiniensis* at Missenden in Buckinghamshire,[82] and to a *Londenestret* at Gamlingay in Cambridgeshire[83] show that London was then regarded as the terminal point of distant roads. So great is the general conservatism of travellers that we may fairly refer the system that we know in the fourteenth century to the Norman period, and indeed beyond.

In the absence of any detailed survey of Norman London, information about the trades and occupations of its citizens can only be obtained incidentally, and from scattered materials. The most important of these materials are private charters relating to transactions in land within the city, for the witnesses to these documents often bear surnames describing their callings or occupations.

Among many names of this type occurring in the early charters of St. Paul's Cathedral[84] may be noted Wulfric tanator, Toli fullo, Sinod scutarius, Aldulf parmentarius, Osmund corduanarius, Ansger sellarius, Wimund loremarius, John coriarius, Robert nebularius, Alwold campanarius.[85] Names like these can be found in most collections of early charters relating to property in ancient boroughs, but the London series is distinguished both by the variety of occupations represented at an early date and by the number of persons following the same calling at the same time. In particular, the number of goldsmiths working in Norman London is very remarkable. The witnesses to an early grant by Bernard son of Ralf the goldsmith to St. Paul's included no less than eight persons following this craft.[86] We also know that a group of London goldsmiths were kept permanently attached to the king's service by a grant of money from the farm of London for the purchase of charcoal. From 1130 onwards, the Pipe Rolls record an allowance of £3 0s. 10d. for this purpose to the goldsmiths, or as they are generally called, "the king's goldsmiths," of London.[87] The goldsmiths were obviously a very important element in the economic life of Norman London, and although the establishment of their Company was still far distant, the fact that eight men of this craft appear together as witnesses to a single charter certainly suggests that some definite and permanent association of the London goldsmiths already existed in the reign of Henry I.

Men of other crafts were already forming such associations in the Norman period. The Pipe Roll of 1130 records a payment of £16 by Robert, son of Leuestan, on behalf of the gild of the London weavers. He was certainly an Englishman by descent, and his appearance as representative of the gild is a good illustration of the native element among the leading men of the city. Between 1154 and 1158, the weavers of London received a charter from Henry II, confirming their gild to them with all the liberties which they had possessed in the reign of Henry I, and forbidding anyone not of their gild to occupy himself in their craft in London, Southwark, or other places belonging to London, save in so far as had been customary in the time of Henry I.[88] For this privilege the king stipulated that the weavers should pay two marks of gold, yearly, at Michaelmas. In the Pipe Roll of 1156 the "bolengarii," or bakers, of London appear as owing a mark of gold for their gild. It is long before there is a similar record of other gilds in London, but in 1180 no fewer than nineteen "adulter-ine" gilds suddenly appear, owing varying sums as amercements because they were formed without war-rant.[89] Most of them are only described by the names of their aldermen, and three of them are called gilds "of the bridge" without further definition. But four of them appear respectively as gilds of pepperers, goldsmiths, butchers, and cloth-dressers, and their existence points, at the least, to considerable activity in association among the members of London crafts in this period. The date at which these gilds arose is a difficult question. The fact that they first appear on the Pipe Roll in 1180 is compatible with a previous existence which may have been long. In any case, it is unlikely that the recorded associations of weavers and bakers were the only gilds which existed in London when Henry II became king.

In dealing with the early history of other English towns, it is rarely, if ever, possible to escape from the atmosphere of legal archæology. It is otherwise with London. Thomas Becket was born there, and among his many biographers, one, William fitz Stephen, prefaced his narrative with a panegyric on the town of his hero's birth, his own city. William's description of London, of which a complete translation is given below, has many claims to a reader's attention. It is an elaborate piece of Latin composition on an unusual theme, it illustrates the social life of a great twelfth century city, and it gives unequivocal evidence as to the importance and general prosperity of London under Henry II. Remarkable as it is, it does not stand quite alone in the literature of its period. In the reign of Richard I, a monk of St. Werburgh's abbey, at Chester, wrote a description of that city which in spirit and general character curiously resembles William fitz Stephen's work.[90] There is an allegorical element in the description of Chester from which William fitz Stephen's writing is free, but each work shows the same pride in the importance of the author's city and delight in its natural advantages. The impression of well-being conveyed by each of these descriptions deserves to be borne in mind in any estimate of the character of English urban society in the twelfth century.

In the case of Chester, there are few materials by which a general description of the city can be tested. The evidence for the history of London in the age of William fitz Stephen is enough to show that his genial vision of the city was not merely the result of unreflecting enthusiasm. It is remarkable how many of the details mentioned by William fitz Stephen are well-known from earlier sources. We cannot, indeed, hope for much information about the sports of the citizens or their customs in regard to marriages and funerals during the Norman period, and descriptions of civic religious observances hardly occur before a later time. But there is no doubt that many external magnates had houses in London, and Henry II himself gave the importance of London as a meeting-place of councils as a reason why bishop Gilbert Foliot should accept translation to that see.[91] There were large houses by the road from London to Westminster already in the time of William I, when Gilbert de Gant gave to Abingdon abbey a *mansio* by the Thames on the way to Westminster from London, with the chapel adjacent to it.[92] Little is known about the early schools of London, but St. Paul's school is mentioned in the Norman period. The original charter is still preserved by which Richard de Belmis, bishop of London under Henry I, gave the *scolae sancti Pauli* to Henry his canon.[93] William fitz Stephen has obviously exaggerated the size of the armies which London had put into the field in Stephen's reign, but it is certain that large forces had really come out from the city during that period.[94] William's observation about the citizens' hunting rights is borne out by the charter of Henry I to the city[95]; by "assemblies on appointed days," William presumably means the meetings of the folkmoot, husting, and wardmoots, and if his reference to the "senatorial order" which existed in London reads like a literary flourish, the archbishop of Rouen could address a highly formal letter to the *senatores incliti* of the city.[96] The naïve exhilaration with which William tells the praises of London somewhat obscures the extent to which they are founded on fact.

It is true that when London is compared with the half agricultural boroughs of the midlands and south, its citizens seem to be living under urban conditions. They themselves were fully conscious of the dangers which attended their habits of life, and used them to support their claims to exemption from participation in inquests taken under oath. "Furthermore, there are many folk in the city, and they are housed close together and are more crowded early and late than other people are, and notably more so than those of the upland, who hold their county court and ought to swear concerning such matters. For if any one in the city should swear against his neighbor, whether concerning an inquest or an assize, or concerning that wherein he has offended, great mischief might arise therefrom; for when the citizens are thus crowded together, whether at their drinking or elsewhere, they might kill each other, and the city would never enjoy steady tranquillity. And for this reason, and by reason of the franchise, and for many reasons, it was established that they should not swear."[97] It is a pretty argument, and that none the less because the citizens were put to inconvenient shifts to excuse themselves from submitting to the new procedure of the inquest. But it does not imply that they lived in a state of extreme congestion. The early survey of the London lands of St. Paul's suggests that a separate piece of London property would possess on the average something between thirty and forty feet of street frontage; and that although the division of these properties into smaller *mansuræ* had already begun, and may have gone far, there was still room for an increased population within the city walls.[98]

It would be an obvious error to regard Norman London as a peaceful city. No town with a large population drawn from many races could have been peaceful under mediaeval conditions. A momentary glimpse of the violence into which Londoners might break out is given by an entry in the pipe roll of 1130. At Michaelmas in that year the sheriff of London rendered account of £99 0s. 12d. *pro assaltu navium et domorum Londoniae,* and thirteen persons, including both Englishmen and foreigners, are recorded as implicated in this disturbance. The outbreak which lies behind this entry must have been a riot on a considerable scale. But neither such an incident as this, nor the impression of violence which we instinctively carry back to the Norman age from later records should be quoted in simple disparagement of the men of Norman London. They were proud of their city and its traditions, and tenacious of its privileges against suspicious kings and their baronial castellans of the Tower. No merely law-abiding populace could have maintained the liberties of the city through foreign conquest, the bureaucratic autocracy of Henry I, and the war for the succession which followed his death. It was because they were ready in resort to violence that the men of the Norman age had secured for the city the place which it held in the England of 1154.

The city was to give the best proof of its well-being in the development which came over its conception of its place in the world during the twelfth century. By the year 1200[99] men in London have reached the idea that England, and London as the head of England, should dominate the narrow seas by her trade and her ships. They have found ideas which were ultimately to help in creating the sense of nationality and even that of imperialism. They have attained an international outlook. The London which established the commune, whose privileges are recognised in Magna Carta, has quite escaped from the circle of ideas which confined the men of 1150. It is indeed appropriate that when the first conception of national power, based upon world-wide commerce and the command of the sea, arises in the twelfth century, it should arise among the men of London.

NOTES

1. *Gesta Stephani,* in *Chronicles of the Reigns of Stephen, Henry II, and Richard I* (ed. R. Howlett, Rolls Series, 1886), III, 5, 6.
2. For a writ of William II addressed to the barons of London, French and English, see J. Armitage Robinson, *Gilbert Crispin* (1911), p. 137. For the use of the term late in the twelfth century see Hist. MSS. Comm. 14th Report Appendix Part VIII, p. 216, where certain characters are quoted referring to the acquisition of land in London by the bishop of Lichfield, "with the assent of the mayor and all the barons of the city in the common husting." The barons of the Cinque Ports are a parallel to the barons of London. On *baro* as a term of social currency see my *First Century of English Feudalism* (1932), 85-90.
3. Liebermann, *Gesetze der Augelsachsen,* I, 675.
4. Liebermann, *Gesetze der Augelsachsen,* I, 173; F. L. Attenborough, *The Laws of the Earliest English Kings* (Cambridge, 1922), pp. 156 *seqq.,* where the regulations

which follow are translated. The difficult problem of the nature of this peace-gild belongs to the history of Saxon, not Norman, London, but the possibility that it may have been this body which gave name to the Guildhall should be noted. On the Guildhall see above, pp. 12-13.

5. *Anglo-Saxon Chronicle*, under the year 912.

6. *Ibid.*, under 1097. On this entry see Miss E. Jeffries Davis' article *Trimoda Necessitas*, in *History* (1928), XIII, 33-4. In explaining a late eleventh century annal relating to the south of England, it is safe to take "shire" in the modern sense of the word. In the same volume of *History*, p. 337, Miss Davis showed that land at Alfriston in Sussex needed royal exemption from work on London Bridge. She has since noticed a writ of 1097 (printed in *Essays presented to T. F. Tout*, 1925, p. 50) addressed to the sheriffs of all the counties in which the canons of St. Paul's had lands, exempting those lands "ab omni opere et castelli Londonie at muri et pontis et balii et carreti."

7. Liebermann, *Gesetze*, I, 526.

8. William fitz Stephen. See below, p. 59.

9. *Monasticon* (edn. 1846), I, III.

10.Stubbs, *Select Charters* (Ninth Edition), p. 97; Liebermann, *Gesetze*, I, 486; facsimile and translation in Sharpe, *London and the Kingdom,* I. There is no serious reason for doubting that the text still preserved in the Guildhall is the original writ issued by William I. Its handwriting and appearance are entirely in its favour. In the language, the only form suggesting a later date is the spelling *portirefan* for *portgerefan.* But the contemporary examples of Old English writing are far too few to justify the statement that the form *portirefan* could not have been used in the early part of the Conqueror's reign. The question of the date of the charter has recently been raised by the discovery of fragments of the royal seal, once appended to it. The seal belongs to the later of two types used in the Conqueror's reign, and shows that the charter cannot have been issued immediately after his coronation. But it may have been issued as early as 1068 (see

Professor Tait's note in *History,* XIII, 279-80) and this date would agree well with the character of the charter itself.

11. Liebermann, *Gesetze,* III, 276, choosing an impersonal phrase, represents the dual of the original by "Bistum und Stadt."

12. William of Poitiers, *Gesta Willelmi Ducis* (ed. J. A. Giles, Caxton Soc., 1845), p. 147: Dies aliquot...morabatur Bercingis dum firmamenta quaedam in urbe contra mobilitatem ingentis ac feri populi perficerentur." It is clear that more than one castle was raised in London at this time.

13. See below, p. 49, and, for the sites, pp. 82-83.

14. Henry of Huntingdon, *Historia Anglorum* (Rolls series, 1879), *sub anno.*

15. The history of the castles in the west is complicated by a charter of Henry I to Richard (the First), bishop of London, mentioning the *fossatum* of the king's *castellum,* near St. Paul's. This is printed in full in *Mun. Gild.,* II *(Liber Cust.),* i. 340, and imperfectly by Dugdale, *Hist. of. St. Paul's* (1658), p. 197. Its date must fall between 1108 and 1122; it probably belongs to 1114, when the king is known to have sailed from Portsmouth, where it was issued. The passage about the *castellum* reads: "tantum de fossato mei castelli ex parte Tamesis ad meridiem quantum opus fuerit ad faciendum murum ecclesiæ, et tantum de eodem fossato quantum sufficiat ad faciendum viam extra murum, et ex altera parte ecclesiæ ad aquilonem quantum praedictus episcopus de eodem fossato diruit." In this context, "ex parte Tamesis," clearly means "on the Thames' side of St. Paul's cathedral"; but the northern boundaries indicated cannot be brought into line with those of Baynard's Castle, and it is probable, as Miss E. Jeffries Davis has suggested, that the *castellum* of this charter really means the walled enclosure of London itself.

16. There is no direct evidence as to the date when the fortress afterwards known as Montfichet Castle was founded, but on all grounds it is probable that like Baynard's Castle and the Tower it belongs to the Conqueror's reign. It certainly existed before 1136, for its

lord was concerned in the plea about the lordship over the water of Thames which cannot be later than that year. It is worth noting that William de Munfichet and Robert fitz Richard of Baynard's Castle attest Henry I's charter to London.

17. Ed. R. Howlett, in *Chronicles of the Reigns of Stephen, Henry II, and Richard I* (Rolls Series), III. 338.

18. The significance of this passage in general and the name "Clarreaux" in particular were first brought out by Round in his article on The Family of Clare, *Archæological Journal,* September, 1899 p. 6. He had previously noted the identification of the Clarreaus with the Clare family in the pedigree of the latter house facing p. 473 of his *Feudal England* (1895).

19. Printed by Matthew Parker, *De Antiquitate Brittanicæ Ecclesiæ,* edn. 1605, p. 118. The writ is bilingual, and the *ministri* of the Latin version is represented by *wicnæres* in the English.

20. The French text of the claim is given in *Munimenta Gildhallæ* II, *Liber Custumarum,* i, 147. There are English translations *ibid.* ii, 554, and in Stow's *Survey of London* (ed. Kingsford) I, 62-5, corrected by Kingford, II 278-9. Cf. *Cal. Pat.* 1272-81, p. 98 and *Placita de Quo Warranto* (Record Commission, 1818), p. 472.

21. Addit. MS. 14252, f. 90b, in *Eng. Hist. Rev.* XVII, 486; cf. above, note 20.

22. Henry of Huntingdon, *Historia Anglorum* (ed. T. Arnold, Rolls Series, 1897), p. 278.

23. Liber L, ff. 47-50b: facsimile in *Descriptive Account of the Guildhall* by J. E. Price (1886); printed by the late Professor H. W. C. Davis in *Essays in Mediaeval History presented to Thomas Frederick Tout,* p. 55-9.

24. The name is interesting as containing the O. E. *gang,* here, presumably, meaning "watercourse," a word which is very rare in local compounds.

25. The survey only mentions twenty, but it relates to the lands of St. Paul's alone, and does not necessarily cover the whole city. The marginal numbers in Davis' edition do not correspond to anything in the manuscript.

26. Bateson in *Eng. Hist. Rev.* XVII, 502.

27. Already in Alfred's time the word *folcgemot* was used to describe the public assembly in which a merchant must produce the men whom he has brought with him. (Liebermann, *Gesetze*, I, 69). This law is of general application, but doubtless referred to London among other places. The word is not infrequently used for a public meeting in later Old English laws, though London seems to be the only place in which it became attached to a particular assembly.

28. The word was applied, for example, to the assembly of pirate crews in which archbishop Alphege was martyred in 1012.

29. This is a record of gifts to Ramsey Abbey by "Athelgiva" (Æthelgifu) wife of ealdorman Æthelwine of East Anglia. It cannot be dated with any precision but probably comes from approximately the year 990. The text is printed in the *Chronicon Abbatiæ Ramesiensis* (ed. W. D. Macray, Rolls Series, 1886), p. 58, and by Kemble, *Codex Diplomaticus*, No. 973. As we only possess a translation of the original Old English, it is possible that the reference to the husting may be an interpolation, but the authority of the Ramsey *Chronicon* is, in general, good. A document of 1032 of which the Old English text is preserved *(Cod. Dip. No. 745)* speaks of 180 marks of white silver *be hustings gewihte*, where the reference is doubtless to the husting of London, though the city is not named.

30. For the "four benches of the hundred," see Round, *Eng. Hist. Rev.* X, 732. In late medieval times, the husting was considered to rank as a shire court as the wardmoots counted as hundred courts. No doubt the arrangement of suitors in four benches was once common to all forms of local assembly.

31. Cases are noted by H. W. C. Davis, *Essays ... presented to Thomas Frederick Tout*, p. 48.

32. *Eng. Hist. Rev.* XVII, 487-8. For the wards of Norman London see above, pp. 9-10.

33. See the note in Kingsford's edition of Stow's *Survey*, II, 337, and Stow's own observations, *ibid.*, I, 292.

34. Many early sources give the name as *Aldermannesberie*. The genitive singular suggests that this *burh* belonged to a single alderman, and I took the name in this way in the first edition of this paper. But the publications of the English Place-Name Survey have shown that it was commoner than used to be thought for a genitive singular to replace a genitive plural temporarily, in names of this type. There can be no doubt that a derivation from ealdormen in the plural, makes the name much more intelligible, and gives due weight to the situation of the Guildhall.

35. *Burh* in London names is recorded by some scholars as virtually equivalent to "house." It really refers, not so much to a house itself, as to the fortified enclosure in which it stood. See below, pp. 18-19.

36. The survey of the London property of St. Paul's Cathedral, already referred to, mentions incidentally *terra Gialle*. For the identification, see Round, *Geoffrey de Mandeville*, p. 436. It is placed beyond doubt by similar forms in later records.

37. Nearly the whole of our information about this gild is derived from the muniments of the priory of the Holy Trinity, Aldgate. Important extracts from these, including the documents relating both to the foundation and to the gift of the knightengild, were copied in the fourteenth century into the City's Letter-Book C, and are printed in full in R. R. Sharpe's *Calendar*, pp. 73-5, 216-25. C. Gross had already used the actual grant of the gild property: see *The Gild Merchant* (1890), I, 187-8. Stow derived his account of the episode, concluding with a translation of the grant (*Survey*, I, 122; cf II, 286, where his errors are corrected by Kingsford) from a cartulary he called "Lib. Trinitate," compiled by Thomas de Axebrigge in the fifteenth century. There is a transcript of this in the Guildhall Library, MS. 122, and the original is at Glasgow: see J. Young and P. H. Aitken, *Catalogue of the MSS in the Library of the Hunterian Museum in the University of Glasgow* (1908), p. 158, for description and former owners. Translations of some extracts are given in *Monasticon* (edn. 1846), VI, 155

seqq. Various original charters to the priory are in the Public Record Office, where there is also an exemplification of a number of early royal writs (on Cartae Antiquae Roll N). The full publication of these scattered materials would throw much light on the early topography of London, and would place the documents which refer to the *cnihtena gild* in their proper context. (E. J. D.)

38. Egerton MS. 3031, f. 64.

39. In virtue of which the Prior of the Holy Trinity ranked as an alderman of London until after the dissolution of the Priory in 1532.

40. On which see Gross, *op. cit.*

41. The social position of the pre-Conquest *cniht* is discussed in my *First Century of English Feudalism,* with reference to the various gilds known to have been formed by men of this class in towns.

42. Printed by Somner, *Antiquities of Canterbury* (1640), p. 365, and by Gross, *Gild Merchant,* II, 37.

43. The predecessors of the great lords who held property in London in the Norman period, on whom see pp. 15-16.

44. In Winchester the bishop's soke is recorded in the twelfth century: B.M. Addit. MS. 33280, p. 228.

45. Translated, with an introduction by Round, in the *Victoria History of Surrey,* Vol. I.

46. Edward the Confessor, e.g., granted sake and soke to Chertsey in a writ addressed to the Bishop and Portreeve of London: *Monasticon,* I, 430.

47. *Index Locorum to the Charters and Rolls in the British Museum,* Vol. I, article London.

48. *Eng. Hist. Rev.* XVII, 484.

49. *Essays ... presented to Thomas Frederick Tout,* p. 57.

50. *Eng. Hist. Rev.* XIV, 428.

51. *Eng. Hist. Rev.* XVII, 492.

52. *Ibid.* XVII, 487, 492-3.

53 Containing the well-recorded Old English word, *port,* "town," familiar in such compounds as "port way," – not, as Stow believed, the Latin *porta.*

54. Pipe Roll Society, N. S. Vol. 5, p. 6.

55.*Ibid.* N. S., Vol. 8, pp. 165, 166.

56. The final *n* of Portsoken preserves the original termination of the O.E. word *socn.* It does not affect the meaning of the name.

57. Birch, *Cartularium Saxonicum,* No. 1288.

58. The *burhgeat* of the text generally quoted under the title, "of People's Ranks and Law" (Stubbs, *Select Charters,* 9th edition, p. 88), clearly refers to the gate of one of these private defensible enclosures.

59. On the urban *burh* see W. H. Stevenson, *Eng. Hist. Rev.* XII, 491.

60. As distinct from the hedged enclosure, the *haga,* of which there are traces in the city in such names as Bassishaw, cf. Kingsford in *Survey,* II, 335-6, 340.

61. For such lists, chiefly, it seems, founded on undated charters, see Newcourt, *Repertorium,* Vol. I, or Hennessey, *Norman Repertorium.*

62. *St. Paul's MSS.,* p. 61. It is worth noting that Thured and Thurgund are both Scandinavian names, and as such are exceptions to the general character of London nomenclature. Thedebald may be either English or continental.

63. Ædwin canonicus, Ædmund canonicus, Æilward canonicus filius canonicus, Siredi, Leuegar canonicus et cantor appear among the witnesses to Thurgund's character quoted above, p. 20.

64. Liebermann, *Gesetze,* I, 524-6; Stubbs, *Select Charters,* 9th edition, pp. 129-30. See also H. G. Richardson, "Henry I's Charter to London," *Eng. Hist. Rev.* (1927), XLII, 80-87.

65. On the financial relation between London and the Crown in the eleventh and twelfth century see Tait, "The Firma Burgi and the Commune in England, 1066-1191," *Eng. Hist. Rev.* XLII, 321-59.

66. See above. p. 3.

67. *Commune of London,* p. 117.

68. Harl MS. 1708, f. 113b.

69. *Historia Novella,* ed. Stubbs, in William of Malmesbury, *Gesta Regum* (Rolls Series, 1889), II, 576.

70. A twelfth century copy of this letter occurs in Egerton MS. 3031, f. 49b. There is a thirteenth century text in Harl. MS. 1708, f. 113, from which the letter was quoted by Round in *Geoffrey de Mandeville*, p. 116.

71. Liebermann, *Gesetze*, I, 498.

72. *Monasticon*, I, 300.

73. Homo Londoniarum non judicetur in misericordia pecuniæ nisi ad suum were, scilicet ad c solidos. (Stubbs, *Select Charters*, ninth edition, p. 130).

74. *Eng. Hist. Rev.* XVII, 499.

75. William fitz Stephen: see verses below, p. 54-55; cf. p. 66, n. 47.

76. Round, *Calendar of Documents preserved in France* (P.R.O., 1899) No. 109.

77. *Ibid.*, Nos. 1375, 1352.

78. Liebemann, *Gesetze*, I, 232.

79. See above, pp. 30-31.

80. The best account of the geographical conditions governing the growth of London will be found in the introduction to the *Report of the Royal Commission on Historical Monuments, London*, Vol. III. It relates primarily to the Romano-British period, but the facts with which it deals changed very slowly. There is a good summary in the London Museum Guide, No. 3, *Roman London*.

81. This is found in the fourteenth century map of Britain in the Gough manuscripts in the Bodleian Library.

82. *Monasticon*, VI, 548.

83. *Index Locorum to the Charters and rolls in the British Museum*, I, 548.

84. Printed or given in abstract in *St. Paul's MSS*.

85. Tanner, fuller, shield-maker, tailor, cordwainer, saddler, lorimer, currier, wafer-maker, bell-founder.

86. *St. Paul's MSS.*, p. 61.

87. There is no definite evidence as to the number of these king's goldsmiths, but in 1194 one of them, Robert Brito, was disseized of his inheritance by the king, and the annual grant to the goldsmiths was reduced by 7s. 7d. It is worth noting that within two pence this amounts to an eighth of the total sum allowed to the king's goldsmiths.

88. A facsimile of this charter, which is the oldest document relating directly to the history of a City Company, forms the frontispiece to Vol. I of *The London Weavers' Company*, by Miss Frances Consitt (1933). A text and translation of the charter are given in the same volume, pp. 180-181.

89. Pipe Roll Society, Vol. 29, pp. 153-4.

90. This important work, *Liber Luciani de Laude Cestrie*, was edited, with the omission of homiletic matter, by Miss M. V. Taylor for the Lancashire and Cheshire Record Society in 1912.

91. Quoted from the *Materials for the History of Thomas Becket* (Rolls Series, 1875-85), V, 25-6, in *Victoria History of London*, I, 178. See below, pp. 55-56.

92. *Chronicon Monasterii de Abingdon* (Rolls Series, 1858), II, 15-16.

93. *St. Paul's MSS.*, p. 29. To the other two schools named by William (see below, p. 51) may be added one at St. Mary-le-Bow *(de Archa)*: see a deed of Henry of Blois in Round, *Commune of London*, p.117.

94. See below, p. 50, and above, pp. 9-10.

95. See below, p. 59, above pp. 20-22.

96. See below, p. 55; above, p. 24.

97. *Eng. Hist. Rev.* XVII, 720 (Miss Bateson's translation).

98. *Essays ... presented to Thomas Frederick Trout*, pp. 55-59.

99. For this date see Liebermann in *Eng. Hist. Rev. XXVIII*, 733.

A DESCRIPTION OF LONDON

BY

WILLIAM FITZ STEPHEN

THE LIFE OF SAINT THOMAS,
ARCHBISHOP AND MARTYR

PROLOGUE

To the Glory of Almighty God and in everlasting
memory of the Blessed Thomas, and for the
profit and edification of all who read or hear me, I,
William, son of Stephen, have been at pains to write
the life and passion of Thomas himself, the good
Archbishop and Martyr. I was his fellow-citizen,
his clerk and a member of his household, and by
his own lips I was called to partake in his anxiet-
ies. I was draughtsman[1] in his chancery, subdeacon
in his chapel when he celebrated, reader of letters
and instruments when he sat to hear suits, and
in some of these, when he himself so ordered,
advocate. I was present with him at the Council of
Northampton, when matters of great import were
transacted, I beheld his martyrdom at Canterbury,
and very many other things herein set down I saw
with my own eyes and heard with my own ears,

47

while certain things I heard from relaters who had knowledge thereof.

Plato in a discourse set forth a form of constitution, Sallust in his *History*[2] described the situation of Africa on the occasion of the Carthaginians' rebellion against the Romans and of the Romans' oft crossing of the seas for their subjugation, and I shall describe the situation and the constitution of London on the occasion offered me by the Blessed Thomas.

A DESCRIPTION OF THE MOST NOBLE CITY OF LONDON

Among the noble cities of the world that are celebrated by Fame, the City of London, seat of the Monarchy of England, is one that spreads its fame wider, sends its wealth and wares further, and lifts its head higher than all others. It is blest in the wholesomeness of its air, in its reverence for the Christian faith, in the strength of its bulwarks, the nature of its situation, the honour of its citizens, and the chastity of its matrons. It is likewise most merry in its sports and fruitful of noble men. Of these things it is my pleasure to treat, each in its own place.

There "the mild sky doth soften hearts of men,"[3] not that they may be "weak slaves of lust,"[4] but that they may not be savage and like unto beasts, nay, rather, that they may be of a kindly and liberal temper.

In the Church of St. Paul is the Episcopal See. Once it was Metropolitan, and it is thought that it will be so again, if the citizens return to the island, unless perchance the Archiepiscopal title of the Blessed Martyr Thomas and the presence of his body[5] preserve that honour for all time at Canterbury, where it now resides. But since St. Thomas has adorned both these cities, London by his rising and Canterbury by his setting, each city has, in respect of the Saint himself, something further that it may urge, not without justice, one against the other. Also as concerns Christian worship, there are both in London and the Suburbs thirteen greater Conventual churches, and a hundred and twenty-six lesser Parochial.

On the East stands the Palatine Citadel,[6] exceeding great and strong, whose walls and bailey rise from very deep foundations, their mortar being mixed with the blood of beasts. On the West are two strongly fortified Castles, while thence there runs continuously[7] a great wall and high, with seven double gates, and with towers along the North at intervals. On the South, London was once walled and towered in like fashion, but the Thames, that mighty river, teeming with fish, which runs on that side with the sea's ebb and flow, has in course of time washed away[8] those bulwarks, undermined and cast them down. Also up-stream to the West the Royal Palace[9] rises high above the river, a building beyond compare, with an outwork and bastions, two miles from the City and joined thereto by a populous suburb.

On all sides, beyond the houses, lie the gardens of the citizens that dwell in the suburbs, planted with trees, spacious and fair, adjoining one another.

On the North are pasture lands and a pleasant space of flat meadows, intersected by running waters, which turn revolving mill-wheels with merry din. Hard by there stretches a great forest with wooded glades and lairs of wild beasts, deer both red and fallow, wild boars and bulls.[10] The corn-fields are not of barren gravel, but rich Asian plains such as "make glad the crops"[11] and fill the barns of their farmers "with sheaves of Ceres' stalk."[12]

There are also round about London in the Suburbs most excellent wells, whose waters are sweet, wholesome and clear, and whose "runnels ripple amid pebbles bright."[13] Among these Holywell, Clerkenwell and Saint Clement's Well are most famous and are visited by thicker throngs and greater multitudes of students from the schools and of the young men of the City, who go out on summer evenings to take the air. In truth a good City when it has a good Lord![14]

This City wins honour by its men and glory by its arms and has a multitude of inhabitants, so that at the time of the calamitous wars of King Stephen's reign[15] the men going forth from it to be mustered were reckoned twenty thousand armed horsemen and sixty thousand foot-soldiers.[16] The citizens of London are everywhere regarded as illustrious and renowned beyond those of all other cities for the elegance of their fine manners,[17] raiment and table. The inhabitants of other towns are called citizens, but of this they are called barons.[18] And with them a solemn oath ends all strife.[19]

The matrons of London are very Sabines.

In London the three principal churches,[20] to wit the Episcopal See of the church of Saint Paul, the church of the Holy Trinity, and the church of Saint Martin,[21] have famous schools by privilege and in virtue of their ancient dignity. But through the personal favour of some one or more of those learned men who are known and eminent in the study of philosophy there are other schools licensed by special grace and permission.[22] On holy days the masters of the schools assemble[23] their scholars at the churches whose feast-day it is. The scholars dispute, some in demonstrative rhetoric, others in dialectic. Some "hurtle enthymemes,"[24] others with greater skill employ perfect syllogisms. Some are exercised in disputation for the purpose of display, which is but a wrestling bout of wit, but others that they may establish the truth for the sake of perfection. Sophists who produce fictitious arguments are accounted happy in the profusion and deluge of their words, others seek to trick their opponents by the use of fallacies. Some orator from time to time in rhetorical harangues seek to carry persuasion, taking pains to observe the precepts of their art and to omit naught that appertains thereto. Boys of different schools strive one against another in verse or contend concerning the principles of the art of grammar or the rules governing the use of past or future.[25] There are others who employ the old wit of the cross-roads in epigrams, rhymes and metre; with "Fescennine License,"[26] they lacerate their comrades outspokenly, though mentioning no names; they hurl "abuse and gibes,"[27] they touch the foibles of their comrades, perchance even of their elders with Socratic wit, not to say "bite more keenly even than Theon's tooth,"[28] in their "bold

dithyrambs."[29] Their hearers "ready to laugh
their fill,"[30] "with wrinkling nose repeat the loud
guffaw."[31]

Those that ply their several trades, the vendors of
each several thing, the hirers out of their several
sorts of labour are found every morning each in their
separate quarters and each engaged upon his own
peculiar task. Moreover there is in London upon the
river's bank, amid the wine that is sold from ships
and wine-cellars, a public cook-shop.[32] There daily,
according to the season, you may find viands, dishes
roast, fried and boiled,[33] fish great and small, the
coarser flesh for the poor, the more delicate for the
rich, such as venison and birds both big and little. If
friends, weary with travel, should of a sudden come
to any of the citizens, and it is not their pleasure to
wait fasting till fresh food is bought and cooked and
"till servants bring water for hands and bread,"[34] they
hasten to the river bank, and there all things desirable
are ready to their hand. However great the infinitude
of knights or foreigners that enter the city or are about
to leave it, at whatever hour of night or day, that the
former may not fast too long nor the latter depart
without their dinner, they turn aside thither, if it so
please them, and refresh themselves, each after his own
manner. Those who desire to fare delicately, need not
search to find sturgeon or "Guinea-fowl" or "Ionian
francolin," since all the dainties that are found there
are set forth before their eyes.[35] Now this is a public
cook-shop, appropriate to a city and pertaining to the
art of civic life. Hence that saying which we read in
the *Gorgias* of Plato,[36] to wit, that the art of cookery is a

counterfeit of medicine and a flattery of the fourth
part of the art of civic life.

In the suburb immediately outside one of the gates
there is a smooth field, both in fact and in name.[37]
On every sixth day of the week, unless it be a major
feast-day on which solemn rites are prescribed, there
is a much frequented show of fine horses for sale.
Thither come all the Earls,[38] Barons and Knights who
are in the City, and with them many of the citizens,
whether to look on or buy. It is a joy to see the ambling
palfreys, their skin full of juice,[39] their coats a-glisten,
as they pace softly, in alternation raising and putting
down the feet on one side together; next to see the
horses that best befit Esquires, moving more roughly,
yet nimbly, as they raise and set down the opposite
feet, fore and hind, first on one side and then on the
other; then the younger colts of high breeding, un-
broken and "high-stepping with elastic tread,"[40] and
after them the costly destriers of graceful form and
goodly stature, "with quivering ears, high necks and
plump buttocks."[41] As these show their paces, the
buyers watch first their gentler gait, then that swifter
motion, wherein their fore feet are thrown out and back
together, and the hind feet also, as it were, counterwise.
When a race between such trampling steeds is about to
begin, or perchance between others which are likewise,
after their kind, strong to carry, swift to run, a shout
is raised, and horses of the baser sought are bidden to
turn aside. Three boys riding these fleet-foot steeds, or
at times two as may be agreed,[42] prepare themselves
for the contest. Skilled to command their horses,
they "curb their untamed mouths with jagged bits,"[43]

and their chief anxiety is that their rival shall not gain the lead. The horses likewise after their fashion lift up their spirits for the race; "their limbs tremble; impatient of delay, they cannot stand still."[44] When the signal is given, they stretch forth their limbs, they gallop away, they rush on with obstinate speed. The riders, passionate for renown, hoping for victory, vie with one another in spurring their swift horses and lashing them forward with their switches no less than they excite them by their cries. You would believe that "all things are in motion," as Heraclitus maintained, and that the belief of Zeno was wholly false, when he claimed that motion was impossible and that no man could ever reach the finish of a race.[45]

In another place apart stand the wares of the country-folk, instruments of agriculture, long-flanked swine, cows with swollen udders, and "woolly flocks and bodies huge of kine."[46] Mares stand there, meet for ploughs, sledges and two-horsed carts; the bellies of some are big with young; round others move their offspring, new-born, sprightly foals, inseparable followers.

To this city, from every nation that is under heaven, merchants rejoice to bring their trade in ships.

"Gold from Arabia, from Sabaea spice
And incense; from the Scythians arms of steel
Well-tempered; oil from the rich groves of palm
That spring from the fat lands of Babylon;
Fine gems from Nile, from China crimson silks;
French wines; and sable, vair and miniver
From the far lands where Russ and
    Norseman dwell."[47]

London, as the chroniclers have shewn,[48] is far older than Rome. For, owing its birth to the same Trojan ancestors, it was founded by Brutus before Rome was founded by Romulus and Remus. Wherefore they both still use the ancient laws and like institutions. London like Rome is divided into wards. In place of Consuls it has Sheriffs every year; its senatorial order and lesser magistrates; sewers and conduits in its streets, and for the pleading of diverse causes, demonstrative, deliberative and judicial, it has its proper places, its separate courts. It has also its assemblies on appointed days.[49] I do not think there is any city deserving greater approval for its custom in respect of church-going, honour paid to the ordinances of God, keeping of feast-days, giving of alms, entertainment of strangers, ratifying of betrothals, contracts of marriage, celebration of nuptials, furnishing of banquets, cheering of guests, and likewise for their care in regard to the rites of funeral and the burial of the dead. The only plagues of London are the immoderate drinking of fools and the frequency of fires.

To that which I have said this also must be added, that almost all Bishops, Abbots and Magnates of England are, as it were, citizens and freemen of the City of London, having lordly habitations there, whither they repair and wherein they make lavish outlay, when summoned to the City by our Lord the King or by his Metropolitan to councils and great assemblies, or drawn thither by their own affairs.

Furthermore let us consider also the sports of the City, since it is not meet that a city should only be useful and sober, unless it also be pleasant and merry. Wherefore on the seals of the High Pontiffs down to the time when Leo[50] was pope, on the one side of the signet Peter the Fisherman was engraved[51] and over him a key stretched forth from heaven as it were by the hand of God, and around it the verse, "For me thou left'st the ship; take thou the key."[52] And on the other side was engraved a city with this device, "Golden Rome."[53] Also it was said in praise of Cæsar Augustus and Rome,

> "All night it rains; with dawn the shows return.
> Cæsar, thou shar'st thine empery with Jove."[54]

London in place of shows in the theatre and stage-plays has holier plays wherein are shown forth the miracles wrought by Holy Confessors or the sufferings which glorified the constancy of Martyrs.

Moreover, each year upon the day called Carnival – to begin with the sports of boys (for we were all boys once) – boys from the schools bring fighting-cocks to their master, and the whole forenoon is given up to boyish sport; for they have a holiday in the schools that they may watch their cocks do battle. After dinner all the youth of the City goes out into the fields to a much-frequented game of ball. The scholars of each school have their own ball, and almost all the workers of each trade have theirs also in their hands. Elder men and fathers and rich citizens come on horse-back to watch the contests of their juniors, and after their fashion are young again with the young; and it seems that the motion of their natural heat is kindled by the contemplation of such violent motion and by their partaking in the joys of untrammelled youth.

Every Sunday in Lent after dinner a "fresh swarm of young gentles"[55] goes forth on war-horses, "steeds skilled in the contest,"[56] of which each is "apt and schooled to wheel in circles round."[57] From the gates burst forth in throngs the lay sons of citizens, armed with lance and shield, the younger with shafts forked at the end, but with steel point removed. "They wake war's semblance"[58] and in mimic contest exercise their skill at arms. Many courtiers come too, when the King is in residence; and from the households of Earls and Barons come young men not yet invested with the belt of knighthood, that they may there contend together. Each one of them is on fire with hope of victory. The fierce horses neigh, "their limbs tremble; they champ the bit; impatient of delay they cannot stand still."[59] When at length "the hoof of trampling steeds careers along,"[60] the youthful riders divide their hosts; some pursue those that fly before, and cannot overtake them; others unhorse their comrades and speed by.

At the feast of Easter they make sport with naval tourneys, as it were. For a shield being strongly bound to a stout pole in mid-stream, a small vessel, swiftly driven on by many an oar and by the river's flow, carries a youth standing at the prow,[61] who is to strike the shield with his lance. If he break the lance by striking the shield and keep his feet unshaken, he has achieved his purpose and fulfilled his desire. If, however, he strike it strongly without splintering his lance, he is thrown into the rushing river, and the boat of its own speed passes him by. But there are on each side of the shield two vessels moored, and in them are many youths to snatch up the striker who has been sucked down by the stream, as soon as he emerges into sight or "once more bubbles on the topmost wave."[62] On the bridge and the galleries above the river are spectators of the sport "ready to laugh their fill."[63]

On feast-days throughout the summer the youths exercise themselves in leaping, archery and wrestling,[64] putting the stone, and throwing the thonged javelin beyond a mark, and fighting with sword and buckler. "Cytherea leads the dance of maidens and the earth is smitten with free foot at moonrise."[65]

In winter on almost every feast-day before dinner either foaming boars and hogs, armed with "tusks lightning-swift,"[66] themselves soon to be bacon, fight for their lives, or fat bulls with butting horns, or huge bears, do combat to the death against hounds let loose upon them.

When the great marsh that washes the Northern walls of the City is frozen, dense throngs of youths go forth to disport themselves upon the ice. Some gathering speed by a run, glide sidelong, with feet set well apart, over a vast space of ice. Others make themselves seats of ice like millstones and are dragged along by a number who run before them holding hands. Sometimes they slip owing to the greatness of their speed and fall, every one of them, upon their faces. Others there are, more skilled to sport upon the ice, who fit to their feet the shin-bones of beasts, lashing them beneath their ankles, and with iron-shod poles in their hands they strike ever and anon against the ice and are borne along swift as a bird in flight or a bolt shot from a mangonel. But sometimes two by agreement run one against the other from a great distance and, raising their poles, strike one another. One or both fall, not without bodily hurt, since on falling they are borne a long way in opposite directions by the force of their own motion; and wherever the ice touches the head, it scrapes and skins it entirely. Often he that falls breaks shin or arm, if he fall upon it. But youth is an age greedy of renown, yearning for victory, and exercises itself in mimic battles that it may bear itself more boldly in true combats.

Many of the citizens delight in taking their sport with birds of the air, merlins and falcons and the like, and with dogs that wage warfare in the woods. The citizens have the special privilege of hunting in Middlesex, Hertfordshire and all Chiltern, and in Kent as far as the river Cray. The Londoners, who are called Trinobantes, repulsed Gaius Julius Cæsar,[67] who "…rejoiced to make no way save with the spilth of blood."[68] Whence Lucan writes, "To the Britons whom he sought, he showed his coward back."[69]

The City of London has brought forth not a few men who subdued many nations and the Roman Empire to their sway, and many others whom valour has "raised to the Gods as lords of earth,"[70] as had been promised to Brutus by the oracle of Apollo.

"Brutus, past Gaul beneath the set of sun,
There lies an isle in Ocean ringed with waters.
This seek; for there shall be thine age-long home.

Here for thy sons shall rise a second Troy,
Here from thy blood shall monarchs spring, to
   whom
All earth subdued shall its obeisance make."[71]

And in Christian times she brought forth the great Emperor Constantine[72] who gave the city of Rome and all the insignia of Empire to God and the Blessed Peter and Silvester the Roman Pope,[73] to whom he rendered the office of a groom, and rejoiced no longer to be called Emperor, but rather the Defender of the Holy Roman Church. And that the peace of the Lord Pope might not be shaken with the tumult of the noise of this world by reason of his presence, he himself departed altogether from the city which he had conferred on the Lord Pope, and built for himself the city of Byzantium.

And in modern times also she has produced monarchs renowned and magnificent, the Empress Matilda, King Henry the Third,[74] and Blessed Thomas, the Archbishop, Christ's glorious Martyr, "...than whom she bore no whiter soul nor one more dear"[75] to all good men in the Latin world.

NOTES

General Note on Text

William fitz Stephen (or Stephanides, as he is sometimes called) wrote a clear, vigorous and highly rhetorical Latin. If his rhetoric is at times apt to cause amusement to a modern reader, it must on the other hand be remembered that he was merely following the precepts of the Schools in employing a style descended from the flamboyant "Asiatic" rhetoric of the first and second centuries A.D., and still clearly recognisable, despite change of outlook, idiom and grammar. He was also well-read, as his quotations and adaptations of the Classics prove. But he is not exceptional in this respect. Such quotation is a commonplace of the literary Latin of the day, and his range of reading in the Ancient poets is typical of his age. References to his sources appear in the following notes.

William fitz Stephen's *Descriptio Londoniæ* was written before the death of the young king Henry, 1183: see p. 60. It was first printed by John Stow, at the end of his *Survey of London* (1598); subsequent editors of that work, especially Strype (1720) and Kingsford (see the note in his edition, 1908, II, 387-8) introduced modifications from various manuscript versions. The copy in the City's *Liber Custumarum* was published in *Mun. Gildhallae* (Rolls Series, 1860), vol. II, pt. i. There are several other editions, including two giving the "Description" in its proper context, the Life of Becket: by J. A. Giles, *Vita S. Thomae (Patres Ecclesiae Anglicanae* series, 1845), vol. I, and by J. C. Robertson, *Materials for the History of Thomas Becket* (Rolls Series, 1878), vol. III.

The present translation is based upon a re-examination of the following original MSS:

The Marshall MS. (75) in the Bodleian; thirteenth century: (M).

The Douce MS (287) in the Bodleian, thirteenth century: (D).

The *Liber Custumarum* in the Guildhall; early fourteenth century: (C).

The Lansdowne MS (398) in the British Museum; early fifteenth century: (L).

Of these *D* is incomplete, beginning *-dacius dente rodant* (see below, n. 29), while *D* and L alone contain the *Vita S. Thomae*. *MD* divide the work into sections with headings, which can hardly be the work of the author, both headings and divisions showing a marked lack of intelligence. C likewise has divisions and headings, both much improved. But C is suspect on other grounds (see below), and the fact that L gives no headings suggests that these may have been absent from the original.

These MSS. present an interesting textual problem of which no certain solution is possible. But examination points to the following conclusion.

M and *D* are closely related, though not actually copied from the same MS. Between them they give a satisfactory text presenting little difficulty save in one instance (see below, n. 39).

C has certain marked differences from the preceding. But in two cases (see below, nn. 29 and 66) the scribe has undoubtedly emended the text because he found the original unintelligible. In four other cases (see below, nn. 7, 21, 23, and 35) he lays himself open to the same charge, though with less certainty, and it is hard to resist the suspicion that in C we have an edited text. In one passage (see below, n. 39) it preserves or restores the true reading (at any rate, in part). It is more closely related to *D* than to *M*, since it twice goes wrong where *D* is corrupt (see below, nn. 29 and 66).

L is nearly related to *MD*, but (apart from minor divergences) at times seems to alter the text in the interests of greater classicism (see below, nn. 22, 34, 61, and 64). It has, however, in one instance clearly preserved the true reading (see below, n. 24) and perhaps in a second (see below, n. 17), while it alone contains one remarkable passage (see below, n. 19). Despite its faults it is possible that L preserves traces of an ancient relative of *MD*, which was, moreover, not divided into sections with headings.

Stow's text (in his *Survey of London*) is derived from a MS. of the same class as *MD*, but not either *M* or *D*, though, like *D*, it clearly showed some corruption of *dithyrambis* (see below, n. 29). He made, it would seem, a few alterations of his own, but these are of very minor importance. The text given by Kingsford, in his edition of Stow, is not that of his author. Further it is uncritical, and his notes as to readings are not always accurate.

A selection of the more important readings is given in the notes below to illustrate what has been said above and to give some indication of the text used for this translation.

INDIVIDUAL NOTES

1. "Draughtsman." For the Latin *dictator* there is no exact equivalent. Probably the composer of the set periods in which the formal parts of episcopal letters were expressed. (F.M.S.)
2. A reference to the *Republic* of Plato and to the *Jugurtha* of Salust, neither of which authors had been read by fitz Stephen. Sallust does not describe the situation of Africa, and the Numidians are not Carthaginians.
3. Lucan VIII 366 (slightly altered).
4. Cp. Persius V. 58.
5. et praesentia corporis *ML: om C.*
6. The Tower of London.
7. intercontinuante ML: intercontinuante spatio C; an unnecessary addition to the detriment of the sentence.
8. abluit *L:* alluit *MC.*
9. Palace of Westminster.
10. taurorum *MC:* ursorum *L.*
11. Virgil, *Georgics* I. 1.
12. Virgil, *Georgics* II. 517.
13. Anon., perhaps by fitz Stephen himself.
14. A hit at Henry II. Cp. the pointed reference to his son "Henry III" above, p. 60.

15. sub rege Stephano *M:* rege Stephano *C:* iubente rege Stephano *L.*
16. See above, pp. 9 and 33.
17. lautiorum *L:* locutione *MC.* The reading of *L* is very close to that of *MC,* and gives the sense "fine manners." "mensae locutione" is odd Latin for "table talk" and spoils the balance of the sentence. But "lautiorum" may be no more than an emendation.
18. See above, p. 2.
19. "The inhabitants...ends all strife." This passage occurs only in *L.* (See p. 5.)
20. See pp. 32-33 and 83-84.
21. "To wit...St. Martin." The passage occurs only in *C.* (See p. 23.)
22. alicuius uel aliquorum doctorum qui secundum philophiam noti et praeclari habentur et aliae sunt ibi scholae de gratia et permissione *MC:* alicuius notorum secundum philosophiam plures ibi scholae admittuntur *L.*
23. conuentus celebrant *ML:* celebrant cum discipulis conuentus gratia exercitationis *C;* the latter reading may be right, but may equally well be an explanatory expansion.
24. rotant *L:* recitant *MC.* That *L* is right is clear from Juvenal VI 449 "curuum sermone rotato/torqueat enthymema." "Enthymeme" – an argument consisting of a single premise and conclusion as opposed to a "syllogism" made up of major and minor premises and conclusion.
25. futurorum *MC:* supinorum *L.*
26. Cp. Horace, *Epistles* II. i. 145.
27. Cp. Macrobius, *Saturnalia* VII. 3.
28. ne mordacius dente rodant *MCL.* There is no MS. support for "uel...rodunt." *D* begins here with "-dacius dente." Cp. Horace, *Epist.* I. xviii. 82.
29. audacibus *MDL:* audacioribus *C:* dithyrambis *ML:* athimaris *(with* ramis *written above) D:* conuitiis *C,* which also has "procaciori" for "Theonino" *(MLD).* The scribe of *C* was clearly confronted with a text in which "dithyrambis" had been corrupted (cp. the reading of *D)* and proceeded to emend it, as he also did with

A Description of London

"Theonino," failing to recognise the quotation from Horace; "audacibus dithyrambis" is also from Horace and undoubtedly correct. (See p. 34.) Stow omits *dithyrambis*, marking the omission with an asterisk. Horace, *Odes*, IV. ii. 10.

30. Cp. Persius I. 132.

31. Persius III. 87.

32. This "cookshop" – for the word *coquina* can hardly mean a "cookshop quarter" – was presumably near the Vintry: the ships would probably come to Dowgate.

33. assa frixa elixa *MD:* frixa elixa *C:* assa pista frixa elixa *L.*

34. panesque *MDC:* panesque canistris *L,* completing the Virgilian line. Virgil, *Aeneid* I. 701.

35. accipienserem...non quaerant *MDL:* accipiunt anserem...non opus ut quid quaerant *C,* an ingenious correction. But that *acipenserem* is the true reading can hardly be doubted. The commonplace Goose is out of place beside these Horatian luxuries, the Guinea-fowl and the Francolin, whereas the Sturgeon is both relevant and Horatian. Horace, *Epodes* II. 53-5.

36. Plato (*Gorg.* 464 B ff.) makes Socrates say that the art of politics (*ciuilitas-politikè*), which has two parts, viz. legislation and justice, attends to the soul, while a nameless art made up of two parts, medicine and gymnastic, attends to the body; flattery has distributed herself into four imitations of these four arts, cookery being the counterfeit of medicine. Fitz Stephen calls it a flattery of the fourth part of *ciuilitas,* as though the four arts together made up *politikè,* the nameless art (of which medicine and gymnastic are subdivisions) being ignored. There is no reason to suppose that fitz Stephen had the least idea of Plato's meaning. His knowledge of the *Gorgias* must have been derived from some Latin allusion to the passage in question.

37. (West) Smithfield.

38. "Earls." The Latin is *Consules,* sometimes used in an Earl's formal style in the twelfth century. (F.M.S.)

39. cute suco satura pilo connitente *C:* succussatura nitente *MDL.* "succusatura" means a "jog-trot" and is

clearly out of place as applied to a "gradarius" ("ambler"). "cute suco satura" is clearly right. But "pilo con-" may be an interpolation, since "suco satura nitente" ("full of glistening juice") is perfectly satisfactory, while "connitente" appears neither in Classical dictionaries nor in Du Cange.

40. Virgil, *Georg.* III. 76.

41. Cp. Virgil, *Georg.* III 84 and 79.

42. bini ex condicto et bini *MDL:* ex condicto et bini *om. C.* The true reading is obviously "bini ex condicto."

43. Cp. Horace, *Odes* I. viii. 6.

44. Virgil, *Georg.* III. 84.

45. Heracleitus of Ephesus (c.510 B.C.) taught that existence was perpetual change; cp. his famous saying, "All things are in a state of flux." Zeno of Elea (c.450 B.C.) sought to prove that on account of the infinite divisibility of space motion was impossible, and that therefore the slowest moving thing (e.g. the tortoise) could not be overtaken by the swiftest (e.g. Achilles).

46. A possible echo of Virgil and Ovid.

47. Anon. A doggerel inspired by Virgil, *Georg.* I. 56 ff. and II.114 ff.

48. Geoffrey of Monmouth, *Hist. Brit.* I. 17.

49. die ius statutis *MDL:* die ius statuendi C. The simplest correction is "diebus statutis." comitia *MDC:* commercia *L.*

50. Leo IX, 1048-1054.

51. All MSS. have "scripto." There is no authority for "sculpto."

52. Cp. Ciaconius, *De Vitis Pontificum* I. 807.

53. Ausonius, *De Claris Vrbibus* I.

54. Virgil; cp. Donatus, *Vita Virgilii* 69.

55. Cp. Horace, *Odes* I. xxxv. 30.

56. Cp. Horace, *Ars Poetica* 84.

57. equus *MDL:* equo *L.* Cp. Ovid, *Ars Amatoria* III. 384. "in gyros ire coactus equus" is in favour of *MDL.*

58. After "cient" *L* adds "et campestria proelia ludunt," a half-line suggested by Hor. *Epist.* I. xviii. 54. Cp. Virgil, *Aen.* V. 674.

59. See note 42 above.

60. Cp. Horace, *Satires* I. i. 114.

61. in prora *MDC*: in celsa puppi *L*, an inappropriate interpolation from Virgil *Aen*. III. 527.

62. Cp. Persius III. 34.

63. See note 28 above.

64. in saliendo in arcu in lucta *MDC*: arcu cursu saltu lucta *L*.

65. Cp. Horace, *Odes* I. iv. 5 and xxxvii. 1.

66. fulmineis *ML* (the last three letters over an erasure in *L*): fulminos *D*: prominentibus *C* (a clear conjecture, the parallel from *Phaedrus* being conclusive for "fulmineis"). Cp. *Phaedrus* I. xxi. 5.

67. Geoffrey of Monmouth, *Hist. Brit*. IV. 3-9.

68. Lucan II. 439.

69. Lucan II. 572.

70. Cp. Horace, *Odes* I. i. 6.

71. Geoffrey of Monmouth, *Hist. Brit*. I. ii.

72. After "Constantinum" *L* inserts "Helene regine filium." For the forged Donation of Constantine see Gibbon, *Decline and Fall*, chapter 49.

73. A reference to the Donation of Constantine.

74. King Henry the third is the "Young King," second son of Henry II. He was crowned at Westminster (1170) and again, with his queen, at Winchester (1172).

75. Horace, *Sat*. I. v. 41.

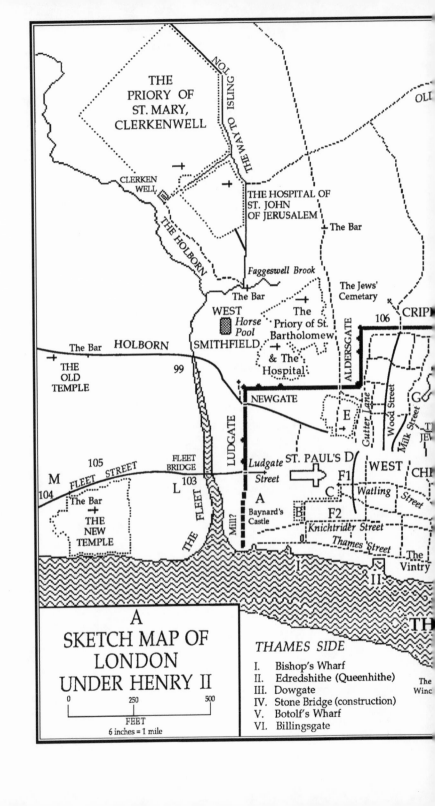

THE
PRIORY OF
ST. MARY,
CLERKENWELL

THE WAY TO ISLINGTON

OLI

CLERKEN
WELL

THE HOLBORN

THE HOSPITAL OF
ST. JOHN
OF JERUSALEM

The Bar

Faggeswell Brook

The Bar

The Jews'
Cemetary

WEST
*Horse
Pool*
SMITHFIELD

The
Priory of St.
Bartholomew
& The
Hospital

106

CRIPI

ALDERSGATE

The Bar   HOLBORN

THE
OLD
TEMPLE

99

NEWGATE

Gutter Lane

Wood Street

Milk Street

G

E

105

FLEET STREET

M

104

The Bar

THE
NEW
TEMPLE

FLEET
BRIDGE

L   103

THE FLEET

LUDGATE

*Ludgate
Street*

ST. PAUL'S D

WEST

CHI

T
JE\

F1

Mill?

A
Baynard's
Castle

B

C

F2

*Watling
Street*

Knichtrider Street

Thames Street

The
Vintry

I

II

TH

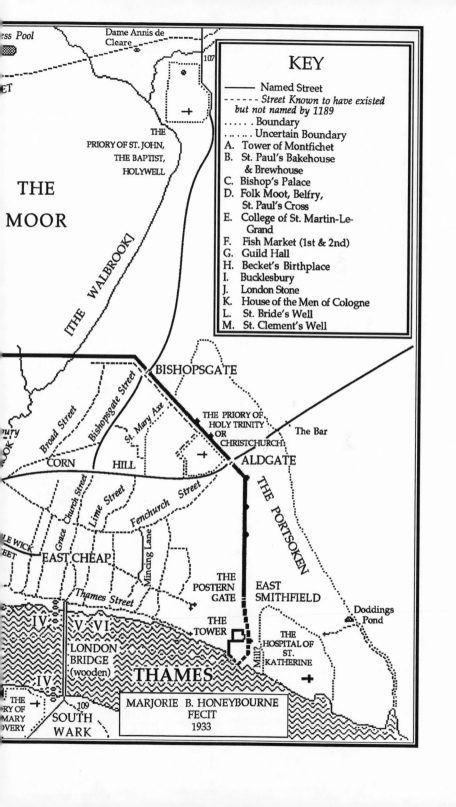

KEY

——	Named Street
- - - - -	*Street Known to have existed but not named by 1189*
. . . . . .	Boundary
. . . . . .	Uncertain Boundary
A.	Tower of Montfichet
B.	St. Paul's Bakehouse & Brewhouse
C.	Bishop's Palace
D.	Folk Moot, Belfry, St. Paul's Cross
E.	College of St. Martin-Le-Grand
F.	Fish Market (1st & 2nd)
G.	Guild Hall
H.	Becket's Birthplace
I.	Bucklesbury
J.	London Stone
K.	House of the Men of Cologne
L.	St. Bride's Well
M.	St. Clement's Well

Dame Annis de Cleare

107

THE PRIORY OF ST. JOHN, THE BAPTIST, HOLYWELL

THE MOOR

[THE WALBROOK]

BISHOPSGATE

Broad Street

Bishopsgate Street

St. Mary Axe

THE PRIORY OF HOLY TRINITY OR CHRISTCHURCH

The Bar

CORN HILL

ALDGATE

Grace Church Street

Lime Street

Fenchurch Street

THE PORTSOKEN

LE WICK EET

EAST CHEAP

Minding Lane

THE POSTERN GATE

EAST SMITHFIELD

Doddings Pond

Thames Street

IV

V VI

LONDON BRIDGE (wooden)

THE TOWER

Mill?

THE HOSPITAL OF ST. KATHERINE

IV

THAMES

MARJORIE B. HONEYBOURNE FECIT 1933

RY OF MARY VERY

SOUTH WARK

109

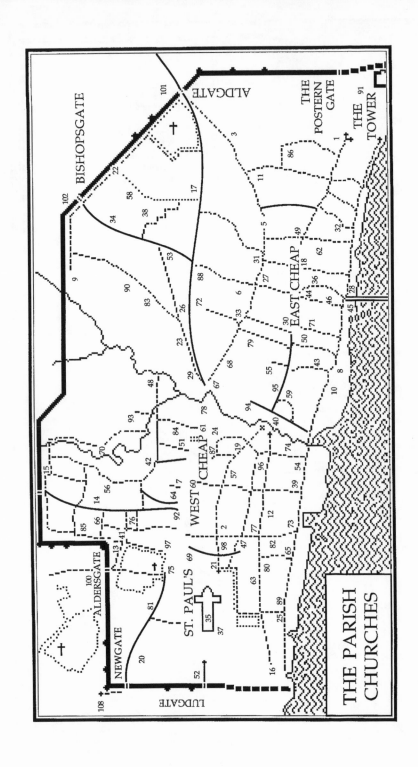

THE PARISH
CHURCHES

Key to the Parish Churches

The earliest form of the name in common use is given; some alternative and later forms, in roughly chronological order, are added within brackets. Modern spelling has been adopted wherever possible. The dates appended are the earliest yet discovered (see Notes to Map). The names of churches which have not yet been found in any document before 1189 are printed in italics. Numbers in parenthesis denote that the church was a peculiar of the Archbishop of Canterbury, not subject to the Bishop of London. The Surrey parishes were in the diocese of Winchester.

Within the Walls

1. All Hallows Barking [Berkingchurch]; before 1148.
(2.) All Hallows Bread Street [Watling Street]; before 1221.
3. All Hallows Colemanchurch [later, St. Katherine Coleman]; c.1180.
4. All Hallows Cornhill – site not found; before 1197.
5. All Hallows Fenchurch [St. Mary or St. Gabriel, Fenchurch]; 1283-4.
(6.) All Hallows towards (or at) Gracechurch [later, Lombard Street]; 1053.
7. All Hallows Honey Lane; 1235.
8. All Hallows the Less [upon the Cellar; near the Ropery]; before 1216.
9. All Hallows London Wall [Broad Street; within Bishopsgate; later opposite the Austin Friars]; c.1108.
10. All Hallows "Semannescyrce," – i.e., Seaman's Church [at the Haywharf; the Great; in the Ropery]; 1106.

11. All Hallows Stainingchurch; 1177.
12. Holy Trinity the Little [the Less; Knightrider Street]; 1266.
13. St. Agnes [St. Anne and St. Agnes; St. Anne Aldersgate]; c.1150.
14. St. Alban; c.1100.
15. St. Alphage within Cripplegate [London Wall]; before 1125.
16. St. Andrew "de Castello" [Castle Baynard; later, by the Wardrobe]; c.1244.
17. St. Andrew on Cornhill [near Aldgate; at Holy Trinity; later, Undershaft]; 12th century.
18. St. Andrew by Eastcheap [Hubbard or Hubert; at the Tower]; 1201-2.
19. St. Antonin [St. Anthony, or Antholin; Budge Row; Watling Street]; 1119.
20. St. Audoen [St. Ouen, or Ewen]; before 1211.
21. St. Augustine by St. Paul [the Little; before St. Paul's Gate; by Distaff Lane; Watling Street; next Old Fish Street; later, Old Change]; 1148.
22. St. Augustine on the Wall [Pappey]; c.1108.
23. St. Batholomew the Little or Less [later, by the Exchange]; c.1150.
24. St. Benet Sherehog [St. Osyth, or Syth]; before 1131.
25. St. Benet on Thames ["super hetham"; Algar; Woodwharf; Paul's Wharf; Castle Baynard]; 1111.
26. St. Benet by Cornhill [later, Fink]; c.1195.
27. St. Benet Gracechurch [Gerschurch; later Langbourne Ward]; c.1181.
28. St. Botolph Billingsgate [at Rethersgate; on Thames]; c.1180.
29. St. Christopher [later, le Stocks]; c.1225.
30. St. Clement Candlewick Street [the Little; Eastcheap; later, Lombard Street]; 11th century.
(31.) St. Dionis [Denis; Lime Street; de Backchurch; de Gracechurch]; c.1200.
(32.)   St. Dunstan in the East [towards the Tower; near Fenchurch]; c.1100.
33. St. Edmund the King; c.1108.
34. St. Ethelburga [many variants]; 1282.

35. St. Faith by St. Paul's [in the Crypt, or Crowdes, of St. Paul's]; c.1150.
36. St. George, Eastcheap [Botolph Lane]; c.1180.
37. St. Gregory "infra atrium" [by St. Paul's]; 1010.
38. St. Helen; c.1162.
39. St. James in the Vintry [on Thames; Garlickhithe]; c.1170.
40. St. John upon Walbrook [the Baptist]; c.1150.
41. St. John Zachary [the Baptist]; c.1150.
42. St. Laurence Jewry; before 1130.
43. St. Laurence next the Thames ["cum cimiterio"; Candlewick Street; London Stone; in the East; later, Pountney or Pulteney]; 11th century.
(44.) St. Leonard Eastcheap [Milkchurch]; 1213-4.
45. St. Magnus "prope pontem" [later, Bridge Street]; 11th century.
46. St. Margaret towards the Bridge ["de froscherch"; near Rethersgate; in Bridge Street; near the Fish-market; later, Fish Street; Crooked Lane]; 11th century.
47. St. Margaret Friday Street [Moses]; 1163.
48. St. Margaret Lothbury; c.1197.
49. St. Margaret Patyns [Pattens; towards the Tower]; before 1216.
50. St. Martin Candlewick Street [Algar, Orgar]; c.1150.
51. St. Martin in the Jewry [the Less; Pomer, Pomery; Ironmonger Lane]; 1176.
52. St. Martin Ludgate [the Little, the Less, Bowyer Row]; 1174.
53. St. Martin Ottewich [Outwich]; c.1217.
54. St. Martin on Thames [Beermanchurch; Vintry]; 11th century.
55. St. Mary Abchurch [Apechurch]; c.1198.
56. St. Mary Aldermanbury; before 1148.
(57.) St. Mary Aldermary; c.1080.
58. St. Mary Axe ["Pellipariorum"]; before 1197.
(59.) St. Mary Bothaw [Bothage; later sometimes corrupted to Botolfe]; c.1150.
(60.) St. Mary-le-Bow; 1091.
61. St. Mary Colechurch; 1176.

62. St. Mary at [up, or de] Hill; c.1190.
63. St. Mary Magdalen [in, or at, the fishmarket; by the west fishmarket; in the new fishmarket; Fish Street; Old Fish Street; Lamberd's Hill]; 1162.
64. St. Mary Magdalen Milk Street ["in foro"]; c.1150.
65. St. Mary Somerset; before 1197.
66. St. Mary Staining ["Stainingehage"; Staining Lane]; 1189.
67. St. Mary Woolchurch [Newchurch; Woolchurch-haw; "Wolmaricherch;" later, at Stocks]; 11th century.
68. St. Mary Woolnoth [Wulnoth Mariecherch]; 1191.
69. St. Matthew Friday Street; 1260.
70. St. Michael Bassishaw [Bassishaghe]; 1187.
(71.) St. Michael Candlewick Street [Crooked Lane; towards London Bridge]; 1271-2.
72. St. Michael Cornhill; 1055.
73. St. Michael Queenhithe [Edredshithe; upon Thames; "super ripam Regine"; "de hutha"]; before 1138.
(74.)   St. Michael Paternoster [later, in the Riole, or Royal; Whittington College]; 1219.
75. St. Michael before St. Paul's gate ["de foro"; "juxta macellum"; le Quern; "ad bladum," at Corn]; c.1130.
76. St. Michael Wood Street [Huggin Lane]; c.1170.
77. St. Mildred Bread Street [Fish Street]; before 1252.
78. St. Mildred "de Walbrook" [near Conyhop; Poultry]; c.1175.
79. St. Nicholas Acon [Candlewick Street; later, near Lombard Street]; 1084.
80. St. Nicholas West Fish Market, or Street [New Fish Market; Coldabbey; behind Fish Street; later, Old Fish Market; near Old Fish Street; Distaff Lane; Cole Abbey]; before 1187.
81. St. Nicholas Shambles ["de westmacekaria"; "apud macellum"; in the Butchery; Aldred; Aldersgate; towards Newgate]; c.1196.
82. St. Olave [St. Nicholas Olave, or Bernard; Bread Street Hill]; before 1188.
83. St. Olave Broad Street, – removed by the Austin Friars, and exact site unknown; 1244.

84. St. Olave in the Jewry [Colechurch Lane; Upwell; later, Old Jewry]; c.1100.
85. St. Olave Monkwell Street [St. Mary Olaf; Silver Street; Cripplegate; near London Wall]; 1181.
86. St. Olave towards [by, or next] the Tower [St. Adulph; later, next the Friars of Holy Cross, or Crutched Friars; towards Aldgate; near Marte Lane; Hart Street]; 1222.
(87.) St. Pancras, Soper Lane; c.1170.
88. St. Peter Cornhill ["binnon Lunden"]; c.1040.
89. St. Peter the Little [the Less; of the Woodwharf; on Thames; Paul's Wharf; later, at Baynard's Castle; near Old Fish Street]; c.1170.
90. St. Peter the Poor, Broad Street; 1181.
91. St. Peter ad Vincula [in the Tower]; 1240.
92. St. Peter in West Cheap [Wood Street; at the Cross of Cheap]; c.1150.
93. St. Stephen Coleman Street [in the Jewry]; c.1181.
94. St. Stephen Walbrook; c.1096.
95. St. Swithun Candlewick Street [later, London Stone]; c.1236.
96. St. Thomas Apostle; c.1150.
(97.) St. Vedast [Faster, Foster; and St. Amandus]; c.1170.
(98.) St. Werburgh [later St. John the Evangelist, Watling Street]; c.1150.

The parishioners of St. Katherine Christchurch [Crichurch, later Cree] worshipped at this time in the priory church of Holy Trinity Aldgate, and those of St. Leonard Foster in St. Martin-le-Grand. Both parishes existed before the Religious Houses in question were founded; their areas extended beyond the precincts.

Without the Walls (*See General Map for these locations.)

99. St. Andrew Holburn [in Portpool]; 10th century.*
100. St. Botolph Aldersgate; before 1135.
101. St. Botolph Aldgate; before 1125.
102. St. Botolph Bishopsgate; c.1213.
103. St. Brigid [Bride]; 1185.*

104. St. Clement Danes; 1135.*†
105. St. Dunstan over against the New Temple [in the West; later, Fleet Street]; 1185.*
106. St. Giles Cripplegate [without the Walls]; c.1090.*
107. St. Leonard Shoreditch; c.1148.*†
108. St. Sepulchre in the Bailey without Newgate [St. Edmund Sepulchre; without Chamberlains Gate; in Smithfield; within the City Liberty]; 1137.

†Outside London. Other Middlesex parish churches (beyond the area included in the map) which William fitz Stephen may have regarded as suburban were St. Margaret Westminster (before 1066; present site 1140); Holy Innocents [later St. Mary-le-Strand; 1143, mentioned earlier as a chapel]; *St. Martin-in-the-Fields* (13th century, probably before 1222); St. Giles of the Lepers [without the City, or in the suburb, of London; later, in the Fields; 1186]; St. Pancras (before 1086); St. Mary Islington (c.1130); *St. Dunstan Stepney* (before 1203).

South of the Thames (*See General Map.)

109. St. Olave Southwark [later, Tooley Street]; before 1085.*

The parish churches of St. George (1122) and St. Margaret (1106) in Southwark were outside the area shown.

Other Surrey churches which may have been regarded as suburban were St. Mary Lambeth (before 1056); St. Mary Magdalen, Bermondsey (before 1086).

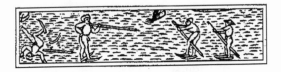

NOTES TO THE MAP OF LONDON UNDER HENRY II

E. *Jeffries Davis*

AND

M. B. *Honeybourne*

The only existing architectural remains of Norman London are the White Tower, the crypt of St. Mary-le-Bow, the choir of St. Bartholomew's Priory church, the round part of the Temple church, and (just outside) the crypt of St. John of Jerusalem: see the Royal Commission on Historical Monuments, London, vols. V *(East London),* IV *(The City),* and II *(West London).* The visible parts of the Wall are mostly Roman *(ibid.,* III, *Roman London,* pp. 83-94), and nearly all the medieval fragments are later than the twelfth century. But the medieval Wall was built upon the Roman, the line of which is, for the most part, known; it has been drawn in our map from Plan A in *Roman London,* the scale being reduced to 12 inches to a mile [six inches to the mile in the maps reproduced here]. This is the same as that of the "Ward Map of the City of London," published by G. W. Bacon and Co., which may therefore be used for exact comparison (e. g., by superposition, with the White Tower and the Cripplegate bastion of the Wall as fixed points) of the topography of the present City with that of Norman London, as here sketched.

The earliest accurate plans of the City are those based upon the official survey, in six sections (apparently not extant), immediately after the Great Fire, finished in December, 1666. The sections were combined in John Leake's "Exact Surveigh of the Streets...contained within the ruines," engraved by Hollar in 1667 (see A. M. Hind, *Wenceslaus Hollar and his Views of London,* 1922, pp. 39-40), a facsimile of which has been issued by the London Topographical Society. In the absence of other evidence this map provides the best material for the ground plan of the medieval city and the position of the churches and other topographical features, and has been used accordingly. A second map of much value for the study of early London is John Ogilby's, on a large scale (100 ft. to an inch) published by Wm. Morgan in 1677: facsimile issued by the London and Middlesex Archæological Society, 1895 (see Hind, *op. cit.,* pp. 41-4). This is the oldest map marking the ward and parish boundaries, and the dimensions of many of the ground plots shown upon it have been found by Miss Honeybourne to correspond with the measurements in medieval documents. The earlier edition of the Ordnance Survey map of the area, on the 25 inch scale, are more useful for historical purposes than that now current: e.g., they give the boundaries of the city parishes, since omitted. There is a copy (1875) in the office of the City Surveyor upon which the present sewers are indicated: this Miss Honeybourne was enabled to consult through the kindness of Dr. A. H. Thomas, Deputy Keeper of the City Records, to whom she is much indebted for help in the research upon which her map is based.

The chief collections of documents relating to the topography of Norman London are the Ancient Deeds at the Public Record Office *(Descriptive Catalogue,* 6 vols., 1890-1915) and the MSS. of the Dean and Chapter of St. Paul's (see above, p. 90). Other deeds are given by N. Moore, *History of St. Bartholo-mew's Hospital* (1918), and E. A. Webb, *Records of St. Bartholomew's Smithfield* (1921). To the relevant secondary works mentioned in Professor Stenton's bibliography, the *Victoria History of Surrey,* vols. I, IV (1902, 1912), and H. A. Harben's useful *Dictionary of London* (1918) should be added, for this purpose. References to original authorities are given below only when it was found necessary to supplement or make more specific those provided by Kingsford (see the Index of Places in his edition of Stow's *Survey,* which may also be made to serve for the *Additional Notes)* and/or by Harben: but many of their references have been checked, and various details corrected.

No place or name is shown on the map unless there is good reason to believe that it existed in 1189; where the evidence is inconclusive or of later date lines have been broken and names printed in italics. The direction of the streets and lanes is given as in Leake's map; no attempt has been made to indicate their width, that being unknown. Where it may be presumed that streets were continued, but the direction is uncertain, the lines terminate with arrowheads. The modern forms of names have been used, except in the cases of West Cheap (Cheapside), and Bassishaw (now Basinghall) and Candlewick (now Cannon) Streets, where the present forms are post-medieval, and the older and more significant are preserved by those of the wards named after the streets. In one case an ancient name, Folkesmares (i.e., folk-boundary), is given, because of its historical interest in connexion with the meeting-place of the Folkmoot.

The Thames is shown 100 feet wider than at present on the northern side: that figure is conjectural, but there is ample evidence in the Husting Rolls and elsewhere (see, for one instance, in 1384, *Archæologia*, LXXIV, 155) that much of the Norman foreshore has since been reclaimed. As there was a riverside embankment along the southern shore by the thirteenth century *(Surrey Archæological Collections,* XXVIII, 153-4) it may be assumed that the line there has changed little. The inlets at Billingsgate and St. Katherine's are both shown on the map by Hoefnagel published in Braun and Hogenberg's *Civitates Orbis Terrarum,* 1572. For the one below, afterwards Hermitage Dock, see the MS. plan of that area, c.1590, lately discovered by Miss Honey-bourne and reproduced by the London Topog. Society. A "tideway" for ships in Southwark is mentioned in Domesday Book (*Vict. Hist. Surrey,* I, 305): probably this was St. Mary Overy's Dock, still a public landing-place.

The upper course of the **Holburn** (hollow burn) is taken from Ogilby's map supplemented for the northern part by the western boundary of the parish of Clerkenwell (see the map published in J. and H. Storer's History of that parish 1828). Below Holborn Bridge the stream's new name and various medieval documents indicate a greater width in Norman times than later, the City Surveyor's map of the present sewers confirms this inference, and shows that the original Fleet was not as straight as the well-known post-Fire "canal."

For the **Walbrook** the ward boundaries have served as the fundamental evidence. The division of the city into wards east and west of that stream, for various administrative and judicial purposes, is mentioned in the thirteenth century and frequently later.[1] Although it was mostly covered by Stow's time (*Survey*, I, 119) he often gives the stream as a boundary in describing the wards. It is clear that when the central wards took permanent shape the Walbrook, being still visible, was used as a division between them. This conclusion is confirmed by the evidence of numerous deeds of the fourteenth century, mostly on the Husting Rolls.[2] The main stream is accordingly drawn along the western boundaries, as given by Ogilby,[3] of the wards of Broad Street, Walbrook, and Dowgate, from the point where it came through the Wall (cf. Stow, *Survey*, I, 175, II, 76-7) to its mouth. But the course thus obtained reaches the Thames some distance to the west of the present Dowgate Dock, where the outfall may often be seen at low tide, flowing over the foreshore under the railway bridge: the mouth of the Walbrook is therefore represented as an estuary, though future research may confirm a suggestion since made by Professor Stenton that it was a delta. Of the two tributaries shown, that on the east was more important outside the Wall than within, for it divided the parish of Shoreditch (named after it) from the Ward of Bishopsgate Without; it survived as a sewer, draining the eastern edge of the "Moor," while the upper part of the Walbrook itself was lost in that marsh. This tributary flows underground along the line of the present Blomfield Street to the Wall; within, it runs under the Carpenters' Hall, and then across Throgmorton Avenue and along Drapers' Gardens to join the main stream. The western tributary runs under the present Guildhall, where its existence is often evident in two places, both on the boundary of Bassishaw Ward. Its exact course has not been worked out: but Stow (*Survey,* I, 290) mentions some grates where the eastern boundary of Cripplegate Ward met the Wall, presumably the place where this stream came through; and, beyond the Guildhall, there is archæological evidence (see *Roman London,* p. 114) that it ran under the southeast corner of Coleman Street. It has been drawn on the assumption that the ward boundaries mark the rest of its course, except for a short distance, where there is a parish boundary. The Walbrook probably had other tributaries but these, for lack of evidence, could not be shown.

The general result differs considerably from that sketched in Plan A, *Roman London* (cf. pp. 15-8, 86-9, 114-8, 171). But the course there suggested was based upon geological as well as archæological evidence, mostly of a date before the establishment of the Roman city, when the basin of the stream had not yet been modified by human agency. Also, during the Roman occupation the volume of water must have been much greater than in the Middle Ages: for some if not all of the culverts made by the Romans to allow the brook and its tributaries to pass through the Wall afterwards became choked, and henceforth the Wall acted as an enormous dam, and the pent-up water formed the **Moor** – William fitz Stephen's "great marsh" (see above, p. 58). The extent of this is roughly indicated by the alluvium shown in the "Drift" map published by the Geological Survey, which also recalls **other Marshes**. There was one east of the Tower, intersected by watercourses,[4] and a second in the valley of the Fleet, – "London fen" in the well known tenth-century charter to Westminster.[5] But these could not be shown on the map for lack of definite evidence, nor could the marshy tract, afterwards occupied by the Austin Friars, north-west of Broad Street, or some others that certainly existed. Similarly, Faggeswell brook, whose course is known, was only one of several **Rivulets**; and there were various **Pools and Wells**, besides those shown: see Stow's *Survey* II, 270-2, 340. The sites of St. Clement's and St. Bride's wells are on the Ordnance map; for Clerkenwell, see *Trans. Lond. and Middx. Arch. Soc.*, new series, vol. V (1923-5); the Horsepool, much smaller than of old *(Survey* I, 16) is on Ogilby's map. The positions of Peerless (or Perilous) Pond, not drained till the nineteenth century, of the well afterwards called Dame Annis de (or le) Cleare, of the pool within the precinct of Holywell, and the holy well itself, are derived from deeds and plans relating to that area collected by Mr. W. W. Braines, who kindly lent his MS. notes supplementing those he used in the *L.C.C. Survey of London,* vol. VIII. Doddings pond, mentioned in connexion with East Smithfield in the description of the bounds of the Portsoken in 1125, and presumably named after the "Dodingus" who held a mill in Stepney at the time of the Domesday Survey, occurs also much later[6]; but its exact site is not indicated in any document we have found. The plan of that region in 1590 shows water in a suitable position: hence the suggestion in the map.

The City Ditch is not inserted: it appears to have been dug in the reign of John,[7] and it is certain that the medieval ditch extended beyond the Roman one (*Roman London,* pp. 94-6), which may have become choked up before the Norman period.

The Bridge has been placed further east than the stone one begun in 1176. It must have remained in use until the other was finished, c.1209, and was probably close by: see *Roman London* p. 47. The position shown in the map was suggested by that of the churches at either end, St. Magnus and St. Botolph on the north St. Olave on the southern shore: all of early date, and one, St. Magnus, described as *prope pontem* long before the stone bridge, which was close to its western end, was built. If the wooden bridge was equally close it must therefore have been east of the church, at the foot of the lane running up to the East Cheap between it and St. Botolph's. This position would coincide with the boundary, south of Thames Street, between those two parishes and also between the wards of Bridge and Billingsgate, which is probably ancient. South of the river the bridge approach would pass immediately west of St. Olave's. A scrap of corroborative evidence from old property lines may be added. There is a plot (acquired by the City, Dr. Thomas informs us, before the end of the sixteenth century) consisting of a strip of land only 40 feet wide, west of the site of St. Olave's, and running straight from the river to the street. It looks remarkably like a bridge both in shape and direction.

A plan of the **Norman Tower of London**, with its *castellum*,[8] is derived from that by A. W. Clapham illustrating his relevant article in *Some Famous*

Buildings (1912); see also *Roman London,* p. 69 and Plan A, and the section on the Tower, with coloured plan, in the *East London* volume. **Baynard's Castle** and the **Tower of Montfichet** are known to have been situated at the south-west corner of the city within the area which afterwards became the precinct of the Black Friars. It may be presumed that the castle occupied most space, that it was next the Thames, and that, as in the case of the Tower of London, the City Wall served as part of its *castellum.* They were separate buildings (see above, pp. 6, 49), and the Tower of Montfichet had a ditch of its own. It may have been the "old and ruined" tower described in 1272 as lying between Ludgate and Castle Baynard.[9] Little has yet been ascertained about **St. Paul's and its Neighbourhood** in the Norman period. The sites of the cathedral and of Paul's Cross shown on the map are those given by F. C. Penrose, in *Archaeologia* XLVII (ii). The plan of the cathedral, as rebuilt after the great fire of 1087, is taken from a reconstruction in MS. (1932; scale 16 ft. to an inch) by R. H. C. Finch, in the Department of architecture, University College, London. The Bishop's Palace was at this time on the south side.[10] No evidence has been found that more than the south-east part of the churchyard had been walled in by the end of the twelfth century. As late as 1321 the citizens declared that the ground immediately west of St. Paul's was a lay fee, belonging to the king, adducing in support of this contention the ancient custom of their musters upon it in time of war, reviewed by the lord of Castle Baynard (see above, p. 7): evidently that open space was still of considerable size.[11] Similarly, they claimed the area northeast of the cathedral (cf. Folkesmares Lane: above, p. 78), the **Meeting-Place of the Folkmoot.** Frequent references to this under Henry III show that it was by Paul's Cross.[12] The Belfry that was used to summon the citizens (later called Jesus Steeple) stood "in the corner of the greater cemetery, towards Cheap."[13]

The site of Paul's Brewhouse and Bakehouse (still marked by a court) was worked out by Miss Honeybourne in her M.A. thesis (1929),[14] where may also be found exact delimitations of the **sites of the Religious Houses** – except Holywell, already dealt with in the *L.C.C.* Survey, VIII, and the Temple, shown on Ogilby's map. She has since published in the *Journal of the British Arch. Assoc.* new series, XXXVIII (1933) an account of the boundaries of St. Martin-le-Grand, the College of secular canons, founded before 1068, which was older than any monastery in or near London except the Benedictine Abbey of Westminster. Next, c.1089,[15] came the Cluniac priory of St. Saviour, Bermondsey; then the three great priories of Augustinian canons, St. Mary Overy, c.1106, Holy Trinity Aldgate, c.1108 (founded by Queen Maud, who was also the founder of the leper hospital of St. Giles, away in the fields), and St. Bartholomew's with its twin foundation, the hospital. The first house of the Knights Templar was built c.1128; the two Clerkenwell houses, St John's and the Benedictine nunnery of St. Mary, c.1130; the hospital of St. Katherine, then connected to Holy Trinity Aldgate, c.1148; the Augustinian nunnery at Holywell before 1158. The site of **Becket's Birthplace** was very near that of the present chapel of the Mercers' Company, which occupies part of the site of the hospital of St. Thomas of Acon, founded in his memory, probably before 1189. The position, only, of **Monastic Churches** is marked by the crosses on the map; no attempt has been made, as for St. Paul's, to draw these in proportion, their size, in the Norman period, being unknown. Those of both the old and new Temples are shown: the latter was consecrated in 1185, its churchyard, apparently, before 1163: see *Geoffrey de Mandeville,* p. 225-6.

No town houses of magnates, except those of the Bishops of London and Winchester, are inserted, because the sites of so few are known that it would be misleading. For similar reasons it was decided not to indicate even the positions of any of the numerous sokes, except the **Portsoken.** There are early delimitations of this *(Cal. Letter-Book,* C pp. 216, 225; cf. above pp. 13-19), but they mention landmarks, e.g. Doddings Pond, not yet identified. It has been assumed that north of the high road the boundary was the same as in Ogilby's time; the line running south to the river has been reconstructed with the aid of the plan of 1590 and other documents relating to the property of the Abbey (fourteenth century) of St. Mary Graces, extending from Tower Hill to the Thames. This area, with those occupied by the enlarged Tower and the precincts of St. Katherine's and the Abbey of Minoresses, ultimately became exempt from the jurisdiction of the City: hence most of the irregularities in the modern boundary of Portsoken Ward.

East and West Smithfield, and the two "cheaps," or **Market-places** are obvious instances of the parallelism between the two parts of London, on either side the Walbrook. Some subdivisions of the western market are shown; others in both, are indicated by the names not only of streets but of churches: cf., in the list of those, nos. 75 and 81 in the west, and in the east nos. 27 (i.e., grass church), 28 (rether=cattle), and 44. The western fish market was moved during the period from one site to another. The first, at the west end of the Cheap (see *St. Paul's MSS.*, pp. 24b, 25a, 26a), is still recalled by Friday Street, not then separated from St. Paul's Churchyard by Old Change, which, like Paternoster Row, was built later. The second (*ibid.*, p. 22) gave its name to the street which ran by the churches numbered 63 and 80. Among other significant suffixes are those of churches nos. 10, 54: the latter was explained by W. H. Stevenson (in an unpublished letter kindly lent by Dr. Page) as the church of the bearers, or wine-porters, of the Vintry. It should be spelt "Bærmannecyrce."

The **sites of the Parish Churches**, shown on the detail map, uniformly indicated by numbers corresponding to those in the Map Key, (their ground plans at this period being unknown), are taken from Leake's map, except St. Stephen Walbrook, which was rebuilt in the fifteenth century on the east side of the street, and St. Alphage, moved in the sixteenth century. The site of St. Faith's may at this time have been outside instead of under the choir of the cathedral. St. Peter in the Bailey, at the date given (see below, no. 91: from *Cal. Liberate Rolls*), was within the walls of the Tower; but it may have existed before they enclosed it. So much rebuilding and enlargement of churches took place later that the sites shown can only be approximate. There is even less finality about the dates given in the list, which should not be used as evidence for the earlier history of London: e.g., no valid conclusion can be drawn from them as to the periods at which different parts of the medieval city were built. Several, it will be noticed, are later than 1189: but the insertion of every church in the map appeared to be justified by the statement in the *Victoria History*, I, 179-80, that all existed before the end of the twelfth century. This was based upon wide research, including manuscript sources, whereas only printed ones were used for her list by Miss Honeybourne. The materials she used are too copious for citation here; all are entered in a register at the Institute of Historical Research. It is hoped that the list may serve as a starting point and through its publication earlier dates may be brought to light. Some have accrued since the map was printed: for nos. 5 and 86 (both c.1200), 17 (1147), 39, 92 (both eleventh century), 28, 87 (both c.1150), 70 (1181), 91 (1237).

NOTES

1. See the references given by W. Page, *London*, p. 194, to which may be added the Calendars of *Mayor's Court Rolls*, p. 155, and *Letter-Book F*, pp. 143-4.
2. Those for the southern area, about the Vintry, have been collected by Mr. V. B. Redstone, who kindly lent his notes; others were examined with the aid of Dr. Thomas who also helped to elucidate the position of the brook and its tributaries with reference to existing streets and buildings.
3. Except by the church of St. Margaret Lothbury, which Ogilby places in Broad Street Ward, while Stow (*Survey*, I, 282) and the O.S. map agree that it is in Coleman Street.

In modern maps the ward boundary lines are straightened out; the actual divisions between properties, and even within buildings (e.g. at 48 London Wall) are significant, though they are rapidly being obliterated by rebuilding.

4. See the plan of 1590 mentioned above, and the documents with which it was found also, for St. Katharine's, P.R.O. List XVI, *Early Chan. Proc.,* ii, 440.

5. Text from the Abbey muniments, Ch. no. V, with translation, in J. A. Robinson's *Gilbert Crispin* (1911), p. 170; cf. his *Flete's Hist. of Westminster Abbey* (1909), p. 12.

6. *Cal Letter-Book* H, p. 46; *Letters and Papers, Hen. VIII,* XVIII, i, no. 623 (43).

7. *Annales Monastici,* ed. H. R. Luard (Rolls Series, 1866), III, 34, 453.

8. See the Appendix "Tower and Castle," in *Geoffrey de Mandeville,* and F. M. Stenton, *The Development of the Castle* (Hist Assoc. Leaftet 22, revised 1933).

9. *Cal. Charter Rolls,* II, 180. If this identification is right, the grant did not take place because the Robert fitz Walter of that day succeeded in establishing a claim to the Tower of Montfichet: see the inquisition quoted by Harben, *Dict. of London,* p. 425 (no. 1034 in *Cal. Inq. Misc.* I). Gervase of Tilbury, in *Chron. R. de Coggeshall* (Rolls Series, 1875), p. 425, and *Cal. Patent Rolls* 1272-81, p. 147 (the same grant as is *Cal. Letter-Book* C, p. 71, and wrongly dated in *Liber Albus, Mun. Gild.* I, 127) should be added to Harben's references.

10. See *Cal. Pat. Rolls* 1401-5, p. 214; *St Paul's MSS.,* p. 27a; and the "Fire Decrees" in B.M. Addit. MSS. 5071, fo. 254; 5073, fo. 212.

11. *Mun. Gildhallae,* II, *Liber Cust.,* i, 343; *St. Paul's MSS.,* p. 49a.

12. *Liber de Antiquis Legibus* (Camden Soc., 1846), pp. 30-46, passim; cf. p. 245.

13. *St. Paul's MSS.,* pp. 26a, 27a, 58b.

14. Summary in *Bulletin of the Institute of Hist. Research,* IX, 25 (June, 1931).

15. See Rose Graham, *English Ecclesiastical Studies* (1929) p. 94.

BIBLIOGRAPHY

Bibliographical Note from the 1934 Edition

Reference should particularly be made to the London records printed by F. Liebermann, *Gesetze der Angelsachsen,* vol. I (1898-1903), especially to the document he entitled *Libertas Londoniensis* (pp. 673-5), to the sections on London and its institutions in vol. II (1906, 1912) of that work, and to the document he edited in the *English Historical Review* XXVIII, 732 (1913); to J. H. Round's studies in *Geoffrey de Mandeville* (1892) and the *Commune of London* (1899), especially to Appendix P in the former work, and to Miss Mary Bateson's discussion, with extracts, of the documents contained in the British Museum Addit. MS. 14252 published under the title, "A London Municipal Collection of the Reign of John," in *Eng. Hist. Rev.* XVII, 480 *seqq.,* 707 *seqq.* (1892). These works are the foundation of the constitutional history of early London. Much information about the city in this age is also contained in collections of records which primarily relate to a later time, but incidentally include early material: such, for instance, as the *Munimenta Gildhallae,* i.e., the City's *Liber Albus* and *Liber Custumarum* (Rolls Series 1859-62, 3 vols. in 4 parts; there is a translation of the *Liber Albus* by the editor, H. T. Riley, 1861); the *Liber de Antiquis Legibus* (Camden Society, 1846; trans by H. T. Riley in *Chronicles of the Mayors and Sheriffs,* 1863); the *Calendars of the Letter-Books of the City of London,* A to C, ed. R. R. Sharpe (1899-1903); and those of the *Early Mayor's Court Rolls* (1924) and *Plea and Memoranda Roll* (3 vols., 1926, 1929 1932), ed. A. H. Thomas. For the topography of the Norman city, see above, pp. 75-77; the chief single source is the report on the MSS. of the Dean and Chapter of St. Paul's in the Appendix to the *Ninth Report of the Hist. MSS. Comm.*, Part i (1883), referred to hereafter as *St. Paul's MSS.* This includes (pp. 60-69) a summary of the cartulary, parts of which have been published elsewhere, known as *Liber L* (cf. p. 1, *St. Paul's MSS.*, and above, p. 39, note 23); but the information given could be greatly increased by the use of other cartularies, not yet accessible in print: especially St. Paul's *Liber A sive Pilosus;* those of Westminster Abbey (see J. Armitage Robinson, *The MSS. of Westminster Abbey*, 1909, p. 93), one of which is now the B.M. MS. Cotton Faustina A. iii; that of St Martin-le-Grand, at the Abbey (16th century transcripts in B.M. MS. Lans. 170, and in the Guildhall Library); that of Holy Trinity Aldgate (see pp. 41-42, note 37); those of St. Mary (B.M. Cott. Faustina B. ii) and St John (ibid., Nero E. vi), Clerkenwell, and that of St Giles of the Lepers (B.M. MS. Harl. 4015). Four of those houses were outside the city, but they had much property there, as had numerous monasteries in other parts of England, recourse to whose cartularies also (many still unprinted) will be necessary before the outline supplied by London materials is completed in any detail. For the early ecclesiastical history see R. Newcourt, *Repertorium Ecclesiasticum Londinense*, vol. I (1708), not superseded by G. Hennessy, *Novum Repertorium parochiale Lond.* (1898), and the valuable article by Joyce Jeffries Davis (Mrs. Dickinson) on Ecclesiastical History, with its accompanying maps, in the *Victoria History of London*, vol. I (1909). The parish churches, 126 in London and the suburbs according to William fitz Stephen, c. 1180 (see above, pp. 32-33, 49), 120 in the city according to Peter of Blois, c. 1199 (*Epistolae*, ed. J. A. Giles, 1847, II, 85; cf. J. Armitage Robinson, *Somerset Hist. Essays*, 1921, p. 134), are the best guide to the early topography: for them see the map above. Like the topography the economic history of the city cannot be adequately known till more early London charters have been printed; but the London moneyers of the Anglo-Norman period are enumerated in the *Catalogue of English Coins in the British Museum, Anglo-Saxon Series*, vol. II, and *Anglo-Norman Series*, vol. I. Contrary to what might have been expected, the latter volume definitely suggests that the relative importance of London as a minting centre declined in the eleventh century. Among the books dealing with London at this period are John Stow's *Survey of London* (first published 1598), ed. by C. L. Kingsford (2 vols., Oxford, 1908, *Additional Notes*, 1927); R. R. Sharpe's *London and the Kingdom* (3 vols., 1894-5); William Page's *London, its Origin and Early Development* (1923); and Martin Weinbaum's *Verfassungsgeschichte Londons, 1066-1268* (Stuttgart, 1929), – the greater part of which, however, relates to the period after 1154. In a later work *London unter Eduard I und II* (Stuttgart, 1933), vol. II, Dr. Weinbaum gives a collection of documents of the thirteenth and fourteenth centuries, many of which throw light upon the earlier period, – beginning (pp. 3-88) with a complete transcription of relevant folios, 88 to 127, of Addit. MS. 14252, including the extracts already printed in *Eng. Hist. Review* XVII by Miss Bateson.

CURRENT BIBLIOGRAPHY

Baker, Timothy. *Medieval London*. London: Cassell, 1970.
Barlow, Frank. *Edward the Confessor*. 2nd ed. London: Eyre Methuen, 1979.
—. *The Feudal Kingdom of England, 1042-1216*. 4th ed. London: Longmans, 1988.
Bates, David. *William the Conqueror*. London: George Philip, 1989.
Bebbington, Gillian. *London Street Names*. London: Batsford, 1972.
Brechin, D. *The Conqueror's London*. Discovering London, no. 2. London: Macdonald, 1968.
Brooke, Christopher N.L. and Gillian Keir. *London 800-1216: The Shaping of a City*. London: Secker and Warburg, 1975.
Brown, Reginald A. *The Norman Conquest*. London; Baltimore, MD: E. Arnold, 1984.
Clark, John. *Saxon and Norman London*. London: Museum of London, 1980.
Davis, R.H.C. *King Stephen*. Berkeley: University of California Press, 1967.
Derwent, K. *Medieval London*. Discovering London, no. 3. London: Macdonald, 1968.
Dolphin, Philippa. *The London Region: An Annotated Geographical Bibliography*. London: Mansell, 1981.
Douglas, David C. *William the Conqueror*. London: Eyre & Spottiswoods, 1964.
Dyson, Tony. *The Medieval London Waterfront*. London: Museum of London, 1987.
Ekwall, E. *Studies on the Population of Medieval London*. Stockholm: Almqvist and Wiskell, 1956.
Falkus, Malcolm E. and John B. Gillingham, eds. *Historical Atlas of Britain*. London: Kingfisher Books, 1987.
Grimes, William F. *The Excavation of Roman and Mediaeval London*. New York: Praeger, 1968.
Haslam, Jeremy. *Early Medieval Towns in Britain, c. 700 to 1140*. Aylesbury, Bucks: Shire, 1985.
Hibbert, Christopher. *London: The Biography of a City*. London: Longmans, 1969.

Holt, J.C., ed. *Domesday Studies*. Woodbridge, Suffolk; Wolfeboro, NH: Boydell, 1987.

Honeybourne, Marjorie B. "Norman London." *London and Middlesex Historian* 3 (1966): 9-15.

—. "The Fleet and Its Neighborhood in Early and Medieval Times." *London Topographical Record* 19 (1947): 13-87.

Lobel, Mary D. and W.H. Johns, eds. *The City of London: From Prehistoric Times to c.1520*. New York: Oxford University Press, 1989.

Loyn, Henry Royston. *The Norman Conquest*. 3rd ed. London: Hutchinson, 1982.

McDonnell, Kevin G.T. *Medieval London Suburbs*. London: Phillimore Press, 1978.

Merrifield, Ralph B. *London, City of the Romans*. London: B.T. Batsford, Ltd., 1983.

Milne, Gustav. *Medieval Waterfront Development at Trig Lane, London*. London: London and Middlesex Archaeological Society, 1982.

Nightingale, Pamela. "The Origins of the Court of Hustings and Danish Influence on London's Development into a Capital City." *English Historical Review* 102 (1987): 559-78.

Pevsner, Nicholas. *The Buildings of England: London*. 2 vols. Hammondsworth: Penguin, 1952, reprint ed. 1973.

Platt, Colin. *The Medieval English Town*. London: Secker and Warburg, 1976.

Poole, Austin L. *From Domesday Book to Magna Carta*. 2nd ed. Oxford: Clarendon Press, 1955.

Reynolds, Susan M.G. *An Introduction to the History of English Medieval Towns*. Oxford and New York: Oxford University Press, 1977.

Rosser, Gervase. *Medieval Westminster, 1200-1540*. Oxford: Clarendon Press, 1989.

Sawyer, Peter. *Domesday Book: A Reassessment*. London and Baltimore, MD: E. Arnold, 1985.

Schofield, John. *Archaeology of the City of London*. London: London Archaeological Trust, 1980.

—. *The Building of London: From the Conquest to the Great Fire*. London: British Museum, 1984.

—, ed. *The London Surveys of Ralph Treswell*. London: London Topographical Society, 1987.

Sharpe, M. "Post-Roman London." *Transactions of the London and Middlesex Archaeological Society,* new series 7 (1973): 353-64.

Smith, Al. *Dictionary of the City of London Street Names.* Newton Abbot: David & Charles, 1970.

Southern, R.W. *St. Anselm and His Biographer.* Cambridge: Cambridge University Press, 1963.

Stenton, Frank M. *William the Conqueror and the Rule of the Normans.* London: Putnam, 1908.

Stow, John. *Survey of London.* Revised ed. London: Everyman, 1989.

Vince, Alan. *Saxon London: An Archaeological Investigation.* London: Sealy, 1990.

Warren, Wilfred L. *Henry II.* London: Eyre Methuen, 1973.

Wheeler, R.E.M. *London and the Saxons.* London: London Museum Catalog no. 6, 1936.

—. *London and the Vikings.* London: London Museum Catalog no. 1, 1927.

Williams, William G. *Medieval London: From Commune to Capital.* London: Athlone, 1970.

Wood, Margaret. *Norman Domestic Architecture.* London: Royal Archaeological Institute, 1974.

GLOSSARY

Abingdon Monastery, a Benedictine Abbey founded c.675 CE, located 6 miles south of Oxford.

Aldgate, the gate at the east of London.

Alfred the Great (849-899), Anglo-Saxon king of the House of Wessex, known for his accomplishments in war, law and education. Consolidated England after the submission of the Angles and Saxons and the defeat of the Danes.

amerced, punished by arbitrary fine.

Anselm (1033-1109), saint, archbishop of Canterbury 1093-1109.

Arthur, a legendary king of Britain who may have had some basis in fact as a sixth-century king of the Britons, son of Uther Pendragon. Led the British army against the invading Saxons c.516; probably won at Mount Badon (c.520) and died at Camlan (537). With his queen Guinevere he is the center of the cycle of Round Table Legends.

Baynard's Castle, on the bank of the River Thames south of St. Paul's Cathedral. The ditch of the royal castle is mentioned in 1111, and the name derives from the Baignards who were dispossessed in 1110. It was destroyed in 1212.

Becket, Thomas (1118-1170), saint; became chancellor to Henry II of England in 1155; archbishop of Canterbury 1162; assassinated as a result of his confrontations with the monarchy.

Bermondsey, a Cluniac priory, in Surrey, south of the Thames opposite the City of London.

Bletchingly, a Norman Castle in Surrey approximately 24 miles south of the City of London.

Canterbury, the principal metropolitan see of England and a significant pilgrimage site in the Middle Ages. Located about 50 miles ESE of the City of London.

castellan, a man who commanded a castle, whether in his own right or as a deputy of a superior.

chapman, a man whose business is buying and selling; a merchant, trader or dealer.

cheap, the place of buying and selling; a market.

Cheap Ward, a ward in the center of London, which included Old St. Paul's.

Chertsey Monastery, a Benedictine abbey founded in the seventh century and refounded in 1110, located 20 miles SW of the City of London.

Chiltern Hills, a line of chalk downs about 30 miles NW of the City of London.

cniht, a boy, youth or lad; a boy or lad employed as an attendant or servant.

Cnut the Great (995/1000-1035), or Canute, the son of Swein Forkbeard, king of Denmark, he took part in his father's invasion of England. In 1014 he was elected king by the fleet but was not recognized as king of England until 1017. He divided the kingdom into the earldoms of East Anglia, Mercia, Northumbria and Wessex, ruling the last himself.

Cray, a river in Kent, which is now at the eastern edge of Greater London.

custumal, a written collection or abstract of the customs of a manor, city or province.

Danegild, an annual tax imposed at the end of the tenth century or in the eleventh century, originally, as is supposed, to provide funds for the protection of England against the Danes, and continued after the Norman Conquest as a land tax.

Domesday Book, "the book of the day of assessment" is the name applied since the twelfth century to the record of the great inquest of survey of the lands of England made by order of William the Conqueror in

1086. It contains a record of ownership, area and value of lands and the number of tenants, livestock, etc.

Ealdred, d. 1069; bishop of Worcester (1044); archbishop of York (1060); crowned William (1066) and Mathilda (1068).

Edward I (1239-1307), king of England 1272-1307.

Edward the Confessor (1002?-1066), last king of the Anglo-Saxon line; son of Ethelred the Unready and cousin of William the Conqueror; canonized in 1161.

Edward the Elder (870?-924), king of the Angles and Saxons, son of Alfred the Great, brother of Æthelflaeda.

Ely Monastery, a Benedictine monastery established by Etheldreda, or Audrey, queen of Northumbria, who became abbess in 673. The present Ely Cathedral is on the site of the monastery structure, which was begun in 1083 and completed in 1106. Located about 65 miles north of the City of London.

Ethelred (968-1016), the Unready, became king of England in 978, bought off Danish and Norwegian invasions; fled to Rouen when Swein was declared king of England, but returned in 1014 to expel Cnut.

Exeter, approximately 170 miles SE of London, it is an ancient city, originally inhabited by the British Dumnonii tribe, and conquered in turn by the Romans, the Anglo-Saxons and the Normans. Site of a Norman castle and a cathedral dating to the Norman period.

Faringdon, the site of a castle in Berkshire 15 miles SE of Oxford, built by Robert of Gloucester in 1144 and destroyed by Stephen in 1145.

folkmoot, a general assembly of the people of a town, city or shire.

gild, a payment or tax.

guildhall, the hall in which a guild met; from its use for a meeting place for the town and corporation often synonymous with town hall.

Harrow, located on high ground north of London; an area of important Saxon settlements; it was the residence of the archbishop of Canterbury, and its hunting grounds attracted poachers as well as guests.

Henry I (1068-1135), king of England (1100-35); fourth son of William the Conqueror and Mathilda; issued the charter that was later the basis of the Magna Carta; conquered Normandy in 1106.

Holy Trinity, priory in the City of London just inside Aldgate, founded by Mathilda, queen of Henry I, c.1108.

husting, an assembly for deliberative purposes, especially one summoned by a king or other leader; a council; a court held in the Guildhall of London by the Lord Mayor, Recorder and Sheriffs.

hythe, a port or haven, especially a small landing-place on a river.

immunist, one who enjoys immunity from the king's or another lord's jurisdiction.

John (1167?-1216), often called John Lackland, king of England 1199-1216, son of Henry II.

Kent, a county ESE of London between the Thames estuary and the Straits of Dover. Inhabited since Paleolithic times, site of Roman settlements. Important area in the Anglo-Saxon period and throughout the Middle Ages.

Lanfranc (1005?-1089) archbishop, opposed marriage of William the Conqueror and his cousin Mathilda, but later was reconciled and counseled William on policy of invasion of England; called to England as archbishop of Canterbury (1070-1089), continued as chief counselor to William; rebuilt cathedral destroyed by fire in 1067; crowned William II (1087).

Lincoln, approximately 90 miles north of London, the site of an important Roman town, one of the major Danish settlements and an important site in the Middle Ages. Its castle and cathedral both date from the Norman period.

Ludgate, a gate at the west end of London on Ludgate Hill.

mansura (mansurae), a manse or city house belonging to a rural estate, usually of an important feudal lord.

masura (masurae), a variant spelling of mansura.

Mercians, inhabitants of the Old English kingdom of Mercia in the middle of south Britain.

Middlesex, an ancient country now part of Greater London. It was settled in the Stone Age, was important in Roman times and became one of the Anglo-Saxon kingdoms.

Montfichet Castle, probably the tower between Baynard's Castle and Ludgate. It existed by 1137.

Normandy, region in NW France bounded on the north and west by the English Channel. It was united with the English kingdom after the Conquest in 1066 by William, Duke of Normandy.

Oxford, 52 miles WNW of London, by the twelfth century it was the site of a castle, abbey and university.

pent-house, a subsidiary structure attached to the wall of a main building and serving as a shelter, a porch, a shed or an outhouse.

portreeve, the ruler or chief officer of a town or borough; after the Norman Conquest often equated with the mayor or holding an equivalent position.

Portsoken Ward, located east of the city from just south of Bishopsgate to the Thames.

Queenhithe (Etheredeshithe), the one harbor above London bridge.

Ramsey Monastery, located approximately 60 miles north of London, a Benedictine abbey established in 969, with a church dating from the Norman period.

Reading Abbey, located 56 miles west of London, a Benedictine abbey founded by Henry I in 1121 and once ranking as third in all England.

Robert, earl of Gloucester (d. 1147), illegitimate son of Henry I and half-brother of Empress Mathilda; quarrelled with his cousin King Stephen; joined with Mathilda in invasion of 1139 contesting royal title.

sac, dispute, case at law, litigation, crime.

Severn Valley, from Plinlimmon in Wales to Shrewsbury to the Bristol Channel.

shrievalty, the office or dignity of a sheriff; a sheriff's jurisdiction or term of office.

soc (sokes), a right of local jurisdiction.

Southwark, located on the south side of the Thames opposite the City of London. Settled in the pre-Roman period.

St. Paul's Cathedral, on Ludgate Hill, legendary but unfounded site of a Roman temple to Diana; site of a Christian church from the seventh century, which burned down in 1087. Its Norman successor was destroyed by fire in 1136 but immediately restored.

Staines, located 24 miles SW of the City of London.

Stamford, approximately 90 miles north of London, the site of Anglo-Saxon, Danish and Norman settlements. Harold, the last Anglo-Saxon king, defeated an invading Norwegian force here in 1066 before turning to meet William of Normandy at Hastings.

Stephen (1097?-1154), sometimes Stephen of Blois, king of England 1135-54, grandson of William the Conqueror; fought against his uncle's (Henry I) wife Mathilda to retain crown and finally acknowledged Mathilda's son, Henry, Duke of Normandy (later Henry II) as his heir.

Surrey, a county SE of London. In Anglo-Saxon times it was held at various times by Mercia and Wessex until invaded by Viking Danes in the ninth century.

Swein or Swegn, also known as Sweyn Forkbeard, father of Cnut (Canute), led or sent expeditions against England periodically from 994 to 1014.

Tower of London, located on the north bank of the Thames at the eastern end of the City of London. The White Tower, the oldest part of the Tower, was built by William the Conqueror.

villanus (villein), one of the class of small farmers in the feudal system; a peasant occupier or cultivator, later entirely subject to a lord or attached to a manor.

Walbrook Ward, located at the center of London around the Walbrook.

Wallingford, approximately 70 miles west of London. The site of a treaty that ended the strife between Stephen and Henry II.

wardmoot, a meeting of the citizens of a ward; especially in the City of London a meeting of the liverymen of a ward under the presidency of an alderman.

were, a man; a male person.

were-gild, the price set upon a man according to his rank, paid by way of compensation or fine in cases of homicide or certain other crimes to free the offender from further obligation or punishment.

William II (1056-1100), king of England 1087-1100, second surviving son of William the Conqueror.

Winchester, 61 miles SW of London, the burial site of many Saxon and Danish kings, including Alfred the Great. The castle and cathedral date from the Norman period. William the Conqueror was crowned here, as well as in London, in 1066.

INDEX

This Book Was Completely Reset on December 31, 2000
at Italica Press, New York, New York & Was
Set in Palatino. It Was Printed
on 60 lb Natural Paper
by BookSurge
U. S. A./
E. U.